PRAI

I DON'T MEAN TO BE RUDE, BUT...

I DON'T MEAN TO BE RUDE, BUT...

SIMON COWELL
with TONY COWELL

EBURY
PRESS

First Published in 2003 by Ebury Press, an imprint of Ebury Publishing

A Random House Group Company

This edition published 2004

Copyright © Simon Cowell 2003

Simon Cowell has asserted his right to be identified as the author of this
Work in accordance with the Copyright, Designs and Patents Act 1988

The Random House Group Limited Reg. No. 954009

Addresses for companies within the Random House Group can be
found at www.randomhouse.co.uk

A CIP catalogue record for this book is available from
the British Library

The Random House Group Limited supports The Forest Stewardship
Council (FSC), the leading international forest certification organisation.
All our titles that are printed on Greenpeace approved FSC certified
paper carry the FSC logo. Our paper procurement policy can be found
at www.rbooks.co.uk/environment

Printed in the UK by CPI Cox & Wyman, Reading, RG1 8EX

ISBN 9780091898281

To buy books by your favourite authors and register for offers visit
www.rbooks.co.uk

INTRODUCTION

Along with 14 million others, I was watching when Will Young was crowned as the first Pop Idol in February 2002. The only difference was that I was ten yards away from Will rather than miles away, and watching him in person rather than on television. And there was also the small matter of what the climax of *Pop Idol* meant to me. I had been part of it long before anyone had heard of Will, Gareth, Darius or even Rik Waller! So maybe I wasn't like those 14 million other people. Maybe I was a little different.

I don't mean to be rude, but ... since the birth of *Pop Idol*, and its explosive success, both here and in America, people have expected nothing less of me. You see, I have become famous for being rude. At first, I was 'the record executive', but in no time I became 'the nasty judge', 'the obnoxious one', or 'the brutal one'. Well, in my mind, I'm the honest one. That's all. On *Pop Idol*, I only ever say what I am thinking at the time. That's the only way I can describe what I'm doing. My statements are genuine. Nothing is rehearsed. When a woman walks in to audition, I might think, 'God, she's ugly.' And this, as luck would have it, is the one show on television where I can actually say to someone, 'God, you're ugly.' To me, it's not being rude. It's being honest. And it's being myself.

Since the show's rise to popularity, I have been asked to be myself in more ways than you can imagine. In America, I have been asked to sing the national anthem at half a dozen baseball games at least – despite the fact that I can't sing a note in tune. I have admitted this on each occasion, only to be told that the crowd wouldn't care less. I have appeared in *Scary Movie 3* as myself. I have even fulfilled a lifelong ambition of doing a voiceover for *The Simpsons*.

Life has also become a little stranger since the show began. One night, not too long ago, I was in a restaurant in Los Angeles having dinner, when I noticed a middle-aged couple looking over at me several times during the meal. As I was leaving, the guy beckoned me over and explained that he and his wife were on holiday. They said they were fans of the show, and I thanked them. Then it transpired that they had more business to discuss. 'Do you do things for money?' asked the man.

'That depends,' I said.

'It's lots of money,' the man said.

'What is it?'

'Well,' the man said carefully, 'I want you to fly to where

I live, come up to my bedroom, and then insult me while I make love to my wife. I'll pay you a hundred thousand dollars.' I declined, but they weren't the only ones. There was the wife of a film producer who wanted me to compliment her while she stood naked by her swimming pool. There was the software mogul who offered me a six-figure sum to walk into his office and tell the staff they were useless programmers. And there was the little girl who begged me to come to her school and tell her art teacher, 'You're ugly!' That one I did consider.

Giving the *Pop Idol* contestants a reality check is part of the entertainment. Without it, the show wouldn't be half as much fun, either for me or the viewers. But there's a more serious side to my frankness. The music industry is a culture awash with sycophants and yes-men. Currently, the record business is harder to break into than ever before. Labels are less willing to invest money in a new artist unless they have something really special to offer – like Justin Timberlake, whose romantic relationship with Britney Spears guaranteed loads of publicity and a surefire road to fame. That's why I prefer to cut through the bullshit. We set out to make a show that honestly reflects the music business. And trust me, the record industry is not particularly nice.

Having bought this book, you are probably already familiar with my personality and the fact that it gets results. I have made millions from taking beginners with raw talent and, through coaching and brutal honesty, turning those hopefuls into global pop stars. With this book, you'll be able to start the difficult but rewarding process of ascertaining whether or not you're one of the lucky few who can make it.

Part of this book is my story. It has to be. I'm enough of an egotist to be honest about that. My story has lessons for anyone who sets his or her sights on fame. I'll take you behind the scenes of the music industry and give you the real scoop on what it takes to make it to the top, either as a pop star, or as a star-maker like myself. Because I'm the ultimate insider on *Pop Idol*, I'll be able to tell you the real truth about what happens backstage on the show: about the rivalries and the alliances; about me and Pete Waterman, Nicki Chapman and Neil Fox. But mainly about me.

Most importantly, I'll share some secrets with you about talent, how to recognize it and how to cultivate it. You'll learn how to develop your skills – assuming you have any to begin with – and how to handle an audition and stand out from the crowd. And I won't hold back when it comes to established pop stars. I'll let you know who are the best and who are the worst, in my opinion, of course. There isn't any substitute for talent, unless, like Enrique Iglesias you have a famous dad – in which case, it doesn't matter that many people think you can't sing particularly well. But even if you have all the talent in the world – and almost no one does – you can't make it to the top without the right guidance. By 'the right guidance', of course, I mean my guidance.

People like to talk about the importance of self-confidence. Believe in yourself, they say ad nauseam. I won't deny that confidence is an important part of stardom. But I believe in something even more important – the 'X Factor'. This is that indefinable quality that sets you apart from the rest of the pack, some of whom can sing, some of whom can dance, and all of whom want to see their name in lights. The X Factor draws people to you and translates into real star power. It's also somewhat beyond your control. Madonna had it, of course, and all the Pop Idols, Will, Gareth and Darius have it. Even though each developed as a talent and gained more confidence as the show progressed, they all possessed an innate charisma that drew the audience to them the moment they started singing. During the audition process for *Pop Idol* what I hope for is to find that person who has the X Factor, and then to help guide them to stardom.

Many celebrities make the fatal mistake of reading their press, absorbing it and changing their ideas about themselves on the basis of what fans and critics say about them. Michael Jackson, if you're reading this book, I'm talking about you. But I'm also talking about me, to some degree. About a month into the first season of *American Idol*, I found that I was a celebrity in ways that I could not have predicted. I was invited onto *The Tonight Show with Jay Leno*. I did the David Letterman show. Wherever I went, I was instantly recognized and mobbed by fans.

Then, partly because I was curious and partly because I am an eternal egotist, I made the mistake of logging on to the *American Idol* website and going to the Judges section, where fans can leave messages for us. Big mistake! Everyone hated me! I began searching desperately to see if anyone had anything nice to say about me. They didn't. I was the most despised man in America. The more I read, the more I began to believe the things that people were saying. Here are a few examples from the website:

To say Simon is just plain mean, is an understatement. I think he's mean, brutal, totally ruthless, and a complete pain in the ass. He's rude, arrogant and way over the top. Let's write to Fox and have him deported to England.

Hey you all, why is Simon Cowell so sarcastic and degrading to just about every contestant on the show? Is he really like this in real life? If American Idol is supposed to be reality TV, then maybe he needs to give himself a reality check – his comments just stink.

Simon, you are the most egotistical, rude, and bad-mannered Brit I have ever heard. Every week you insult the cream of America's home-grown talent. You need to go back to Britain and get a brain scan because you don't know a good singer when you hear one. I hope that some day one of the contestants physically attacks you.

And those were the nice ones!

During filming the following week, I realized that these comments were starting to influence me. In short, I was behaving. I was observing myself at a distance, trying to be more polite than usual, even saying kind things that I didn't mean, but that I rationalized as confidence-boosters for these budding young entertainers. At one point I found myself agreeing with fellow *American Idol* judge, Paula Abdul. That was the last straw. I had committed the cardinal sin in the record industry – I was taking myself too seriously. It was an important lesson; I never logged onto the website again.

In today's celebrity-obsessed world, every youngster wants to be famous. Who wouldn't? The crazy excesses of stars like J. Lo and P. Diddy make for fascinating reading and inspire thousands of would-be pop stars to run out and hire a voice coach. J. Lo, in particular, embodies the pop dream. Her rags-to-riches story proves that anyone can do great things with hard work, talent and a little luck. With charisma, charm and that elusive X Factor, J. Lo has been able to achieve unparalleled success in both her singing and acting careers (*Gigli* aside). And anyone who can make light of herself by saying 'I could serve coffee using my rear as a ledge' is fine by me. If you are an aspiring P. Diddy, however, you should remember that you won't just have to buy nice suits. You'll also have to see to it that your initials are sewn onto every sheet, pillowcase and white suede chair that adorns your home. Sad.

Joking aside, the problem is that most people don't understand that to be successful in the music business you must first have talent. It's not enough to come to an audition with stars in your eyes, dreamily contemplating your inevitable rise to fame. It's not enough to come to an audition with just a costume or an attitude. People will do the strangest things just to hide the fact that they are completely and utterly talentless.

Before the first season of *American Idol* aired, we went to New York for auditions, and the first person through the door introduced himself as 'Milk'. The second I heard that name, I thought to myself, 'OK, we may have a problem here.' Then there was the fact that he looked like Clark Kent – if Clark Kent had been stupid enough to wear a bandanna around his head. First impressions count in this business, you can either confirm them or contradict them, but they definitely count. In this case, he confirmed them. More about him later.

Throughout the auditions in America we've had people turn up dressed as bananas, lizards, wizards, vegetables, and one even came as a Christmas tree. This particular audition finished when the girl plugged herself into the mains and her fairy lights lit up.

The music business is like football. Everyone wants to win the World Cup. But there is a huge difference between playing for your school team and playing for your country. Likewise, there is a big difference between singing along with your guitar in your garage and selling five million albums a year. The problem is that too many people think they're capable of playing in the World Cup, and they're dead wrong.

Let's go back to the X Factor for a moment. Even if you have a voice like Barbra Streisand, you won't get very far if you're essentially ordinary. All the biggest pop stars, from Elvis and the Beatles to Elton John and Madonna, have possessed that elusive X Factor. Frank Sinatra wasn't the best singer; technically there were others with better pitch and range, but he had a particular aura about him. When he walked onstage and tilted his head up towards the microphone, you were transfixed. He had such stage presence. He was a born star. So what is it that made these artists so success-ful? What has helped them sustain their popularity? What set them apart from the wannabes of their time? And why am I the only man on earth who can explain it all to you?

Keep reading.

I Don't Mean to Be Rude, But...
Madonna Doesn't Shock Me Any More

If you're looking for a blueprint for stardom that includes all the ingredients – self-confidence, talent and naked ambition – you don't have to look any further than Madonna. The young Madonna, that is, the Madonna of the early eighties. When she exploded onto the music scene, she could sing and dance just fine, but that wasn't what made her a megastar. In addition to talent, she had an innate ability to know exactly what the market and the media wanted: sex. She possessed it, and she knew how to make everyone else feel like they could almost, but not quite, possess it. It was a tease that was also completely satisfying, and it was a brilliant career. From an insider's point of view, Madonna's approach was interesting. She ignored the traditional approach, which was to work through record companies, and instead decided to take an alternative route. She went directly to the top record producer, Jelly Bean Benitez, who skilfully honed her first hit single, 'Holiday'. Then, armed with a highly polished product, they approached Sire Records and struck a deal. The rest, as they say, is history. Today, though, the Madonna of that era is no more. Ten to fifteen years ago, I could hum along to 90 per cent of her music. Now I can't. And while she used to be a genius of the provocative gesture, today's Madonna – shock-horror – kisses Britney Spears at the MTV Awards. Young people today! If Madonna really believed that kissing the semi-virginal Britney

Spears would increase record sales, she's nuts. I think in her day, Madonna was one of the most innovative artists in the world. She had that in built instinct to know what producers to work with, and how and when to reinvent herself. She is a legend. But now she's a mum and a wife. She's respectable.

1

The first time I was rude to someone I was four years old. Unfortunately, my mum was the victim. It was December 1963, less than a month after President Kennedy had been assassinated in America, and the British government was still reeling from the Profumo call-girl scandal in which top government officials, including John Profumo, the Minister of War, were caught with their pants down.

The mood at home was particularly glum. Dad was a staunch Conservative and, had it not been for his success as an estate agent, he might have gone into politics. As a result, the upheaval in the political world, both at home and in America, upset him greatly. Still, he made it clear to the rest of the family that it was essential, if only for the sake of the children, to continue with our plans for Christmas. This came as a huge relief to me – the thought that anything could possibly hijack my Christmas toy delivery was my first and only concern.

On Christmas Day, Mum was seated in her vast mirrored dressing room, putting the final touches to her make-up. Like many women in Britain at that time, she modelled herself on that quintessential icon of style, Jackie Kennedy. Mum had it down to a fine art: she had the same trim figure, the same raven hair, the same cropped suit and the pillbox hats. That night, the crowning glory of her movie-star outfit was a huge white mink hat.

I was crouching at the foot of the stairs with my new train set. The one highlight of an otherwise dull collection of Christmas presents, it was spread before me on the vast wooden floor as Mum made her entrance down the sweeping grand staircase.

'What do you think, darling?' she asked, stepping cautiously over the railway track. 'Does Mummy look pretty?'

I looked up at her and stared at the furry hat. 'Mum,' I said, 'you look like a poodle.'

I was born in October 1959, into postwar Britain, and grew up in a sizeable home on a small estate in Elstree, north of London. My father, Eric, was a prosperous estate agent and quantity surveyor and my mother was something of a local socialite. I was brought up with three half-brothers:

Tony, John, Michael, my half-sister, June, and my brother Nicholas. We played, we fought, we terrorized each other and the house staff. More of that later. The world I was born into was very different from the way the world is now. We had no McDonald's, no colour television, and, luckily, no Paula Abdul.

The fifties had been an austere period in Britain – there had been lots of belt-tightening after the war, and lots of grey predictions about the economy and the culture. As the sixties dawned, it was the first time teenagers could get decent work and the chance to earn some money. Better still, they could hang onto their teenage dreams, which for many meant forming a pop group. And not an old-style pop group, with barbershop singing. In the sixties, we grew up with proper rock-and-roll groups, smack-dab in the middle of the biggest music revolution the world has ever known.

My early childhood was accompanied by a soundtrack of some of the most exciting music ever produced. Elvis was one of the first rock-and-roll singers I ever heard. The British press at the time referred to him as 'an American teenager throbbing with sex'. And it wasn't only kids that loved Elvis, their mums did, too! Elvis and his management team, including the legendary Colonel Tom Parker, were the first to recognize the power of television as the most powerful method of selling millions of records.

A little later my elder brother, Tony, bought the first Bob Dylan album, which he proceeded to play over and over again while struggling to sing along in Dylan's nasal vocal style. I'm not sure who sounded worse. Today, neither my brother nor Bob Dylan would get through a single audition on *Pop Idol* – at least, not as long as I remain one of the judges. One of them can't sing and the other's too boring. Throughout this era of early rock-and-roll, my parents continued their long-running affair with artists such as Frank Sinatra and Tony Bennett. As a child, these artists did nothing for me, although eventually I came to understand the appeal of Sinatra. One of the world's greatest entertainers.

And then, of course, the Beatles came onto the scene and changed it in ways that no one could have predicted. At the end of 1963 – during the same dismal period I mentioned earlier, when the Profumo scandal was on everyone's mind – the Beatles had hit No. 1 in the pop charts with 'She Loves You', which was also the first record I can remember asking my mum to buy for me. In part, this was because my elder brother, Tony, had it, but it wasn't only a matter of imitation. It was the first time in my life that I had been interested in music; and I was desperate to own a copy. There was something about that music that made me sit up and listen.

At the time, it seemed like a wonderful, peaceful revolution. What I didn't realize then – I was only four years old, after all – is that record companies were the main benefactors of the Beatles' ascendancy. Soon, the British public was bombarded by sound-alike bands like the Hollies and the Dave Clark Five, looking to jump on the bandwagon. The cultural revolution meant big money for someone. And after *Time* magazine coined the phrase 'Swinging London', it was only a matter of time before America got the message, too. The next Beatles record, 'I Want To Hold Your Hand', went to No. 1 in the United States and four other Beatles tracks went simultaneously into the top five slots on the *Billboard* charts.

Rehashing the Beatles' early career may sound like ancient history, in a sense, but it's also important history, because it utterly changed the possibilities for popular entertainers. Not only were the Beatles wonderful singers and increasingly talented songwriters, but they were something else: celebrities at a level for which there was no precedent. The Beatles were also the first band to be photographed living it up in what we now perceive as traditional rock-star fashion. They were seen lounging in the backs of limos, drinking champagne and lording it up in hotel suites. But they were also young and boyish and seemed utterly distinct from the musical acts of previous generations. For the first time young people looked at them and thought wistfully, 'That could be me.'

I was one of those young people.

* * *

I spent my happy childhood, as I have said, growing up in a large country house in Elstree, just twenty miles north of London. Abbots Mead, the house, was in five acres of landscaped grounds. Part of my father's job involved assessing a building site and determining the materials necessary for completing the construction, and he had purchased Abbots Mead as a sad ruin. Convinced he could return the house to its former glory, he spent two years gutting and then rebuilding the interior. The house itself was built on four floors with eight bedrooms, four bathrooms and a ton of places in which to hide and explore. For a naughty four-year-old boy, Abbots Mead was the perfect place in which to grow up.

Life at home was a well-organized affair. Mum was the captain, and she ran a tight and orderly ship. We had a gardener named Robin who pruned and tended the gardens. Mrs Ostler cleaned the house and kept it shipshape. And Heather, our devoted live-in nanny, had perhaps the hardest job of all. Heather looked after the three youngest Cowell children: Tony, Nicholas and me. If we were little devils, Heather was nothing less than an angel. She cooked for us, cleaned for us and even made sure Tony was in bed before two in the morning – he was just entering his trainee rockstar rebellion period, and didn't care for rules and regulations. To this day, she still has a number of mementos from her years with us, including my old pink pram, which she proudly displayed on *This Is Your Life* this year. Thanks Heather!

In those days, Elstree was the Hollywood of the British film industry. It had begun as a sleepy country village, but then, in the early part of the century, two major studios were built there and a town grew up around them and the jobs. Those two studios, MGM and Associated British Picture Corporation, were the home to a string of British-made films, including *Secret Ceremony* with Elizabeth Taylor, *Where Eagles Dare* with Richard Burton, Robert Aldrich's *The Dirty Dozen* and Stanley Kubrick's *2001: A Space Odyssey*. In fact, some years later, Kubrick himself bought Abbots Mead from my parents. According to my dad, who had always been a snob when it came to architecture and interior design, Kubrick ruined the house by turning most of the ground floor into a private cinema.

During my childhood, the stars who worked at Elstree included Roger Moore, Gregory Peck, Robert Mitchum, Bette Davis and Maureen O'Hara. This created a brand new world of celebrity for my parents, and, by extension, for me. The stars soon became our friends and neighbours, and whenever they were in town I got to rub shoulders with the cream of Hollywood, as long as I could squeeze my way past my mum. The leader of this exclusive Hollywood circle was our closest neighbour, Gerry Blatner. Gerry was head of

Warner Brothers Films in the UK, and whenever Hollywood stars came to Elstree they would stay at Gerry's house. The first guest of Gerry's that Mum ever met (over the garden fence) was Bette Davis, who became a regular visitor to the house. There are not many kids who can say that they sat on the knee of Bette Davis while she learned her lines. (Though how she managed to learn her lines at all in the presence of my mum, who could out-talk anyone, remains a complete mystery.)

Roger Moore, best known as James Bond, was another star who was in town quite often. Mum was a big fan of his television show *The Saint*, which had rocketed him to fame, and Roger would often invite us to watch him film the TV show on the back lot of Elstree Studios. By this time Tony was working as a runner on the show, and his job was to drive and position the cars on the set. Often he would let me ride around the studios in the back seat while he drove, as long as I kept my head down – which, of course, I stubbornly refused to do. Other frequent dinner guests were the actor Trevor Howard and his wife, Helen Cherry. Trevor once asked me if I wanted to be an actor when I grew up. 'No,' I replied, bored. 'I don't like actors.'

With Mum so at home with 'theatrical' types – it came from her days on the London stage, she always said – it wasn't long before the Cowell family was enjoying a nonstop whirl of film industry parties, often held at Abbots Mead. My parents entertained with endless cocktail hours and formal dinners. From my perch at the top of the staircase, I used to peek through the rails in fascination at the scantily dressed women sipping champagne. This is an interest, I admit, I have never lost.

Some nights, as the music and laughter increased, I would venture further down the staircase, step by step. I knew that if I attracted the attention of one of the more intoxicated guests I would soon be invited down to join the fun. My dad cut a handsome figure. In fact, with his jet-black hair and stylish suits, he was often mistaken for one of Gerry Blatner's film-star guests. Dad had a wicked sense of humour and would hold court at dinner parties with a nonstop stream of witty anecdotes and rude stories, which he delivered with a deadpan face.

Dad was highly successful in his business and worked hard to make his money. That meant, of course, that he was off to work early each day; every morning at 7.30 a.m. he would jump into his white E-type Jaguar and drive the twenty miles to his London office with the hood down and one of his trademark Cuban cigars in his mouth. With Dad away most of the day, the bulk of our rearing was left to Mum. And since my own disobedient tendencies were apparent from an early age, that meant that Mum had to take a firm hand with me. She was always telling me what to do or what not to do, and I was forever refusing to listen to her.

It is easy, with hindsight, to reflect on how this privileged upbringing and artistically rich atmosphere came to influence my interest in music and films. It certainly gave me confidence at a very early age. Mixing with the cream of Hollywood, I always had a feeling that I would end up working in the entertainment business.

While the Beatles and the Rolling Stones dominated the airwaves during the mid-sixties, my parents hadn't really noticed. The dulcet tones that reverberated down the corridors of Abbots Mead, mostly in the early hours of the morning, belonged exclusively to (yawn) Charles Aznavour, Shirley Bassey, Perry Como and Jack Jones (Mum had the hots for Jack). They were all hugely successful artists, but to a four-year-old, strong-willed little brat, not to mention his teenage older brother, they were just a terrible noise. I may not have been able to read, but I already knew precisely what music I didn't like – and my parents had a sizeable collection of it. My younger brother Nicholas and I would constantly beg Mum to 'turn that rubbish off', and we even began to hide the records we hated most by slipping them under the expansive sofas in the lounge. One day in a fit of pique I actually put a huge scratch across one of Mum's favourite records using one of Dad's screwdrivers. I was determined that I would never have to hear Shirley Bassey ever again.

Tony had been banished to the top floor of the house, as he was in his early teens. It was there, in Tony's smoky bedroom, that I first experienced a wide range of rock and pop stars – Bob Dylan, Neil Young, the Beach Boys and even Tom Jones – and listened to Tony's own painfully pathetic attempts to emulate Jimi Hendrix. It's a shame that I was too young to offer him my informed opinion and guidance.

But my first music lesson at school gave me just that opportunity. As a five-year-old in a rowdy class of twenty other junior Beatles, I was anxious to get my hands on a guitar like Tony's. My po-faced music teacher, Mrs Jones, had other ideas. She made me play the bass drum. Not at all amused by the choice of instrument, I proceeded to bang the drum so hard that it drowned everyone else out. Mrs Jones looked on in horror and promptly swapped my drum for a triangle in a vain attempt to bring some order to the class. I soon realized what a complete and utter racket we were making; it was terrible. I raised my hand and demanded an explanation. 'Miss,' I said, 'this is absolutely dreadful. Why are you making us do it?'

I had no idea back then that this was how I would end up making millions.

Neither did Mrs Jones, who saw to it that I was promptly escorted out of the class and not allowed back. Thank God.

At home I was, like many boys, something of a brat, especially to my younger brother, Nicholas. While I idolized Tony – he was so much older that he seemed to come from another world – Nicholas was only a year and a half younger, which meant that he was almost a kind of twin. This also meant that he was the competition. Before he appeared on the scene, I had been the star. So my main goal, from the time he could walk, was to get him into as much trouble as possible. Luckily for me, Nicholas was more than willing. I soon realized that all the bad things I wanted to do I could get Nicholas to do for me – and also take the blame. Perfect.

Some of the mischief that I remember revolved around Father Christmas. One Christmas Eve, I spotted Dad creeping into our bedroom laden down with sacks full of presents. I had been a cynic since I was seven or so, and I was pretty certain that Father Christmas was just a story adults told to gullible children. When I saw Dad, I knew that I was right, and as soon as he had left the room, I immediately woke Nicholas and spilled the beans. 'Father Christmas isn't real,' I said, 'and the quicker you come to terms with it, the better.' He was in tears and wouldn't believe what I was saying.

The following Christmas, I took a huge collection of pots and pans from the kitchen and balanced them carefully along the top of our bedroom door. Later that night, when Dad crept in with our toy delivery, there was an enormous crash as the kitchenware came raining down on him. Nicholas shot bolt upright in bed and glared at Dad. I turned to Nicholas with a big grin on my face and proudly announced, 'See, I told you, Father Christmas does not exist.' Nicholas burst into tears, and Dad looked sheepish as he left the room, kicking out at the pots and pans that littered the bedroom floor.

Weeks later, to my delight, I discovered Dad's Father Christmas suit hidden in the attic. I couldn't wait to show my little brother. He was devastated. 'Is Santa dead?' he asked.

'Don't be stupid,' I replied sharply. 'He was never alive.' I couldn't believe he was taking so long to get the message. To drive home the point, I suggested that we should set fire to Santa's beard. At first Nicholas didn't want to do it.

'Why should I?' he whined.

'Because Simon says,' I replied with confidence.

We torched the suit. We were in hysterics as thick smoke filled the attic.

Tony was sixteen at the time, and he was supposed to be keeping an eye on the two of us. He smelled the burning suit and came running up the stairs in a panic. He managed to extinguish the fire and was able to save Father Christmas's torso, but sadly not his legs. At least, as we told Mum, the house didn't burn down.

Nicholas was such a willing apprentice that he became a kind of test pilot for all my schemes. One day I decided that he needed a haircut and that I would be the one to give it to him. It was my first attempt at an image makeover. I sat him on a stool in the middle of his bedroom and pulled a big pair of scissors from the drawer. I said, 'Nicholas, that hair has to go', and proceeded to chop off great chunks till the floor was covered with his hair. He looked like a mad monk, his scalp peeking through on the top.

Once I had completed his haircut, Nicholas couldn't wait to go downstairs and show off his new style to Mum. I shall never forget Mum's voice as it thundered through the house: 'WHERE... IS ... SIMON?'

As you might guess, my school days couldn't arrive quickly enough for Mum – she was desperate to get rid of me. Even Heather was looking forward to some deserved rest. I never wanted to go to school. I hated every school I went to. I would do anything to avoid going. All I wanted to do was to stay home and play football.

The two things I hated about school were the discipline and boredom. The discipline I could not tolerate because I thought it was unnecessary. And the boredom of sitting in a classroom attempting to do mathematics, physics or geography was complete torture. I just had this sneaking suspicion that learning about Newton's theory wasn't actually going to play a huge part in my future. The only subjects I enjoyed were soccer, athletics, English and art. And girls.

The first girlfriend I remember was named Amanda. We were at school together, and I used to follow her around like a puppy. Of course, I was only five at the time. My first real kiss came four years later, with a girl who lived near me. Our lawn at that time had three tiers, and if you were on the lowest lawn you couldn't be seen from the house. Her name was Tara and it was a big moment for me when I ended up kissing her.

By the time I became a teenager, girls were my number one obsession. In fact, whether it was because of them or because of the general hormonal rushes of adolescence, I was always in a kind of torment. I think it's fair to say that I was the world's worst teenager. From the age of 15 to 17, I was always running away. Like clockwork, every month or so I would fight with my parents – usually my mum – and then pack a bag with toothpaste and some jeans and a shirt, and head out. And not a small bag, for some reason, but a large, unwieldy suitcase. I didn't have a car, so I would just walk out of the house with my huge suitcase, get about fifty yards from the house, realize I had nowhere to go, and then hide with the suitcase for a few hours. Then, after my mood had blown over, I would creep back into the house, scowling at Mum, who of course knew that she had won the battle.

I lost my virginity when I was 17, to a girl who was attending Windsor Technical College. We had been seeing each other for a while, and she made it clear to me that she wanted to lose her virginity. I played it cool, acted like I was a man of the world, but the truth, of course, was that I was still a virgin also. The night came when we both knew it was going to happen. My parents were out of town, and we planned to go out to the local pub. I had a motorbike then, and we drove from my house down to the pub, which was only about half a mile away, and started to drink. Or rather, I started to drink. She thought I was experienced, but, in truth, I was terrified and I dealt with that by drinking – and drinking and drinking. She kept asking me if we could leave, and I kept saying, 'OK, OK, in a second.' Eventually we got back onto the bike and wobbled up the lane to the house. By the time we got in the front door, her top was off. By the time we reached the top of the stairs, she was completely nude. She asked me to take a bath with her, but after a minute, she jumped out and went to the bedroom. 'Simon,' she said, 'I'm ready.' I remember wishing I could just drown. So I went like a lamb to the slaughter. As it happened, everything worked out fine, but it was the most nerve-wracking experience of my life.

We broke up a little while later, after we went to a dance. It was the college disco night. Of course, since she wasn't a virgin any more, I was completely smitten. She had always been very flirtatious with one of the teachers there; he was a cool-looking guy, and older. I lost sight of her at the party and the next thing I knew she was snogging this teacher during a slow dance. I got back on my motorbike and went home distraught. In fact, I couldn't even sleep. The next day, I called her up and uttered what has to be the most pitiful line in the history of romance: 'Can I have my crash helmet back?'

Like most guys my age, I've had my fair share of girl-friends, but one thing has embarrassed me. It was the story in the papers that quoted me as saying that I had slept with 70 to 100 women. If I had read that about somebody else, I would have thought he was a complete wanker, and there I was, looking like a complete wanker. As it turns out, I didn't boast about it, exactly: I was once asked in an interview to guess how many girls I had slept with. I based my estimate on when I lost my virginity, figured that it was roughly 25 years ago, and guessed that I had slept with an average of three or four women a year. That's how I ended up with the number. I wish I hadn't made that calculation, because it makes me sound like a complete idiot.

I Don't Mean to Be Rude, But...
I Am Slightly Cynical About Marriage

People always want to know why I have never married. Well, part of the problem is the institution of marriage. Some people join up for the right reasons – they want to get married and have kids – but many others do it out of social obligation. They grow up and live in areas where their friends have got married. Dinner parties are always centred around couples, and if you're the odd bloke out you can be ostracized. I've seen that happen time and time again, and marriage is a form of conformity.For me, it's not a problem. Because so many of my ex-girlfriends are still good friends to this day, I've never felt lonely if I'm not in a relationship. I've never felt pressured, or insecure, or worried that I'll end up alone. As far as kids are concerned, I'm brilliant with them, as long as they belong to other people and I don't have to be with them 24 hours a day. I can see them when I want. They're normally in a good mood, they're normally happy to see me, and more importantly I can walk away. Perfect. But on a more serious note, I have always worried that if you're not a parent by your thirties, you're creating a situation where you're a 60-year-old with a teenage son.

The longest relationship I have had so far is two years. I would hate to be part of a couple you see every day in a restaurant who are having dinner but haven't got a word to say to each other.

The current relationship I'm in is an interesting one (every time I say 'current' she kills me). Terri, my girlfriend, has been with me now for just over a year; I met her through an ex-girlfriend of mine called Laura. When we first met, it was about 12 years ago, so she would have been about 17 or 18 at the time. I remember thinking that she was gorgeous, like a little pony – she had long legs, a bit gangly, and I thought she had some growing up to do. But she was always great fun and fantastic company. Then, about seven or eight years ago, we were all at the London club, Tramp. I wasn't with anyone that night and Terri wasn't with anybody either. We were both part of a big group, and we got absolutely plastered and started snogging like mad in the club. I remember thinking two things: a) where did that come from? and (b) that was fantastic. But we didn't follow it up with anything, and I lost contact with her for a couple of years. Then two years ago I ran into her again. When I moved to Los Angeles to do American Idol she was on a modelling trip, and she asked if she could stay at my house. I said sure: I was always having English friends to stay. Her work went well, and she was easy to have around, as a friend, and then one day we just got involved. I'm very comfortable with Terri. We argue like mad, and I think it's one of the reasons why we get on so well, because there's an absence of any icy politeness. I have been shouted and screamed at like I have never been shouted and screamed at in my life.

One night, there was practically an earthquake warning in Los Angeles when she ran into the room to let me know what she thought of me. But I can always make her laugh straight afterwards. She'll be in a bad mood for about half an hour, and then just come straight out of it. She is also incredibly supportive of my work and schedule. She has a natural instinct for a hit and has been very helpful when I am developing new shows. My family love her and I adore her. Who knows…?

Nicholas had been sent away to boarding school, but I was kept at home to attend the local private school. I was thrilled that he had been sent and not me. But, after a few months, the headmaster told my mum that they were going to throw me out of school, so I was packed up and sent to Dover College to join Nicholas. It was harder for me to leave home at that age – I was fourteen or fifteen at the time – than if I had been younger, because I was old enough to know that this wasn't going to be summer camp. I remember arriving at Dover and heading down to the trunk room to put my trunk away, knowing I wouldn't see it again until I went home for the holidays. That was a miserable sensation.

The first night I was there, I was in a melodramatic mood, and I wrote a letter home immediately. It went something like this:

Dear Mum and Dad, I hope you're happy to finally have got rid of me. I also hope you're happy in your centrally heated warm house and you have a lot to eat. Because I am lying in a dormitory which has icicles on the inside, and there is nothing to eat. I'm freezing cold and hungry. I hope you're finally satisfied. Simon.

There were six houses, which were basically big buildings where the boys slept, and the whole experience was a bit like *Harry Potter*. It was boarding school at its worst: the older boys beat up younger boys and there were more rules than I knew what to do with. That was also around the time that co-education was starting to infiltrate the system. We had about three hundred boys, and about six girls, and of course guys at that age would go after anything. Some of these girls weren't exactly beauty queens, but you'd never know it from the attention that they got. I expect they had a rude awakening later on in their lives.

The system was oppressive. I was never caned at school, or beaten by teachers, but at one point I was caught drinking with a bunch of friends at a Dover pub. We technically weren't allowed to leave school, but we would sneak out most evenings. Somehow, a creepy prefect who was there, spotted us and reported us. This guy was pitiful. The next day, I was called in by the housemaster, who told me that he knew I had been there with my friend David, but that they needed the identities of three of the other boys. I refused to give them up. They pressured, and I kept refusing, and in the end I was suspended for five weeks. I was delighted with the five-week holiday, but Mum was furious and she tried to make me do heavy labour at home – chopping down trees, that kind of thing. After a week she gave up and I had a great holiday.

I had only two goals. Number one: smoke as many cigarettes as possible. Number two: leave school at the earliest possible age. A few of us were even put into a special category because we were so useless. We were given the option of either having tutors to improve our grades or learning to play tennis. To this day, tennis is still my best sport. I left school with 2 O levels to my name.

Having fluffed my way through every academic challenge, I finally left school at the age of 16. I went to a technical college in Windsor for a year where I managed to pass one O level, giving me the grand total of three. My prospects looked bleak, and to make things worse I had no idea what I wanted to do with my life. While Mum and Dad had their own ideas of what I should do – including taking an office job or becoming an estate agent – I had no real idea of what I wanted to do. All I did know was that I wanted to make money. Real money. I credit my parents with this: from a very early age, they made us earn our own pocket money. But pocket money wasn't enough. I soon became obsessed with getting rich. From the age of eight I used to make money by cleaning cars on a regular basis. I made quite a lot from this, about £1 a car, and I would do maybe ten cars a day. Later, as I got older, I worked as a babysitter, a window cleaner, a carol singer and a waiter in Elton John's restaurant in London. I think I lasted two days there before being asked to leave – yes, I was the worst waiter in the world. It was clear that waiting tables wasn't the career for me. But what was?

Dear Mr Cowell

Since you like summing up people on PopIdol
I thought you might like a little of your own
medicine.

You can't sing
You're too old
Your smile is insincere
You have terrible dress sense
You don't know what you're talking about.

There, it doesn't feel very nice does it.

Best regards
Mr S

As I considered my future, the one thing I knew for sure was that I couldn't look to my peers for an example. Most of my friends were still in college, or taking a year off to travel the world. For me that was never an option. I had no desire whatsoever to hike across the dusty plains of Australia roughing it as a backpacker. I wanted to earn money, not waste my time.

At this point, my parents were panicking about my future prospects, and they weren't the only ones. Growing up in a celebrity atmosphere had given me a taste for the world of entertainment. But to work in the music industry or films would have been considered just a pipe dream in those days. Particularly as I had no experience or academic qualifications apart from an overdeveloped ego. In hindsight, I was perfectly qualified.

Dad clearly had his own views on what I should do for a living. But they didn't fit with mine. One evening he came looking for me in my bedroom, where I would sneak off to smoke cigarettes and listen to my records. In 1977, punk rock was injecting new energy into the British pop scene, but it left me cold. I was more interested in American pop, in bands like Fleetwood Mac (who had released their immensely popular *Rumours* album) and the Eagles (their song 'Hotel California' became my anthem for the summer).

Dad was on a mission that night, and anxious to pin me down about my future, or lack of it. I didn't hear him enter the room with one of my records blaring from the speakers. He motioned to me to turn down the music, sat down on one of my large yellow bean bags, and almost toppled backwards. I then listened to him (in quiet desperation) as he tried to talk up the same boring career ideas, which involved property or retail. His sermon had the same effect on me as listening to a Perry Como record. Painful.

The following morning, I learned that Dad had come up with a cunning plan to kick-start my career by lining me up with a host of job interviews that he had organized through his business colleagues. I'm sure he meant well, somewhere deep down in the recesses of his heart, but to me those interviews seemed – and still seem – like a particularly sadistic torture regimen. I couldn't avoid them forever, as they were suggested by my parents, who loved me (and were now getting desperate), but I did my best to do my worst at each and every job interview that was inflicted upon me.

Career Number One: Simon the Builder

Dad was a quantity surveyor, and he had had this strange notion that I would benefit by following in his muddy footsteps into the building trade. 'It's better than doing nothing, son,' he used to say. Wrong, I thought.

To keep the peace, I finally agreed to attend a two-day training course to learn about building materials. That was my first big mistake. In the early hours of the morning Dad drove me to Birmingham where the company's training division was based – managed by one of Dad's mates, of course. My poor father spent the whole two-hour car journey vainly attempting to sell me the virtues of a career in the building industry. Cue Perry Como again.

We arrived in Birmingham at 11 a.m. in the pouring rain. I wasn't amused. The place looked like one gigantic building site. I couldn't believe I was there. After wading through the mud and rubble for close to an hour, I had seen enough. I turned to Dad and said, 'Are you completely mad? I am not staying here a minute longer, let alone two nights. You can forget this.'

He looked shell-shocked for a second. 'I take it you are not interested, then,' he replied sarcastically.

'No.' I said. 'Not in a million years.'

We drove home in the Jaguar in complete silence while he puffed and chewed angrily on his cigar.

Career Number Two:
Simon at the Supermarket

My next stop was an interview with Tesco. Once again Dad had a hand in this debacle; he knew one of the top bosses at Tesco, and he was able to get me onto a trainee programme where the pay was quite good. Dad's bogus enthusiasm was hardly contagious. He told me that if I started off as a trainee manager and proved my worth, I could go on to become a regional store manager – whoopee! Still, I did need the money – Dad had stopped his weekly handouts which had fuelled my smoking habit – so I felt resigned to at least take a flier at every single hare-brained career idea that he came up with.

I arrived at Tesco's London headquarters and was quickly ushered into the tiniest office I had ever seen. Behind the desk sat a middle-aged man wearing a grey suit. His hair was combed over his head to hide his bald patch. Before I had time to sit down, he was already looking me up and down disapprovingly.

Finally he said, 'May I ask why you are wearing jeans?'

'Well, I am wearing a jacket,' I replied.

'But why are you wearing jeans?' he repeated.

'I didn't know that a suit was a requirement for the job,' I said.

He just glared at me.

'You do not walk into my office for a job wearing jeans. You're not management potential. I don't want to interview you.'

Now I'd heard enough. 'As a matter of fact, I don't really want to end up as a 50-year-old bore, sitting in an office the size of a telephone booth. So I think we are both happy to end this now.'

As I got up to walk out, he shouted after me, 'You can't talk to me like that, you know.'

'I just did,' I said, slamming the door behind me.

Career Number Three: Civil Simon

The third time around, my dad went completely over the top. Believe it or not, he thought it would be a great idea for me to apply for a job in the Civil Service as a trainee law clerk. (Number one criterion for the job: 'Are you the most boring person in the world?') Quite frankly, it was the most bizarre idea I'd ever heard in my life. By this time I was beginning to get the distinct impression that I was going to have a permanent career attending interviews for the dullest jobs in Britain: all very amusing, but it didn't pay very well.

The day of my Civil Service interview, I sat in a waiting room for what seemed like hours. At some point during this interminable wait, a middle-aged woman handed me a fact sheet illustrating the earning potential within the Civil Service, should I be lucky enough to get through the interview process. Lucky enough? If I joined at 18, I learned, I could earn as much as £12,000 a year by the time I was 65. Twelve thousand pounds a year! There was absolutely no chance that I was going to sit in a stuffy office as a budding law clerk for the next 50 years. Finally, after hours of waiting, I was summoned into a vast room to be faced with a panel consisting of three very stony-faced judges. I think that this is what's known in literature as foreshadowing.

The one female member of the panel, who bore a strong resemblance to *The Weakest Link*'s Anne Robinson, proceeded to ask me a whole host of meaningless questions to which I responded with complete indifference. After a few minutes, she rose from her chair and issued her verdict. 'Mr Cowell,' she said, 'I'm afraid to say that you are the most unsuitable candidate we have ever had the misfortune to interview.' This was music to my ears.

Still intent on having the last word, I turned to face the

judges. 'Thank you all for saving me from a fate worse than death,' I said.

Career Four: Simon on the Big Screen

Some weeks later, after I'd received a rather sulky letter of rejection from the Civil Service, Dad finally conceded defeat in his bid to take my career to new lows. At the same time, he confessed to Mum that he had a sneaking suspicion I had sabotaged every job interview he had sent me to.

Now I decided that it was time to do something about my own career. I knew that without any qualifications I would have to take a job at the very bottom of the ladder. I was interested in film, music and television; I knew that any of these industries would be great fun, and I had a feeling that you could probably make a lot of money. I decided to call my cousin, Malcolm Christopher, who worked at Elstree Studios, and ask if he had any jobs available.

It turned out that Malcolm was the production manager on a new television series, and he quickly agreed to take me on for a three-month trial as a runner. Dad wasn't thrilled, he just grunted and said it wouldn't last. I was beside myself with joy. I wasn't in the Civil Service, or at a building site. Instead, I was working in the same studio where they had shot *Star Wars*.

True, I was making only £15 a week and working from 5 a.m. until 7 p.m. And true, my job wasn't traditionally glamorous. Being a runner meant exactly that – I spent my long days running errands for other people, errands that included buying haemorrhoid treatments for the rather creepy executive producer. Still, I worked like a Trojan. I never stopped running. I was never late and was always friendly to everyone on the set. Everyone liked me, apart from the haemorrhoidal executive producer. I found him a bit arrogant, vain and outspoken, and he spent most of the day strutting around the studio issuing orders while forgetting to use the word 'please'. It sounded like the perfect job.

At the end of my three months, Malcolm went to see the producer, saying, 'Look, we want to keep Simon on – it's only £15 per week and he's worth every penny.' Somewhat predictably, he said no; he said that he didn't have money in the budget to employ a runner.

When Malcolm broke the news to me, I was struck dumb. Malcolm was embarrassed for me. 'Look, Simon,' he said, 'I'll pay the £15 a week out of my own pocket. Just carry on working. But keep your head down when the executive producer is around.' Grateful as I was to Malcolm, this proved easier said than done. It made me nervous, and I would resort to hiding whenever the executive producer showed up on the set. Inevitably, one day he caught me hiding under a desk. He pretended he hadn't seen me but told his secretary to get rid of me; he didn't even have the guts to tell me to my face.

Malcolm was really apologetic, but powerless. So in the end I had to walk. My first concern was my parents. The thought of having to tell Dad I had just been sacked filled me with complete horror. I could just see him smiling as he opened up his little book called *The Most Boring Jobs in the World*. But I always remembered something that my father had told me: tenacity is the maker of dreams, and if you want to succeed at something, you have to persevere. It's a trite lesson, maybe, but no less true for its triteness. I went to see another producer friend of Malcolm's, who seemed to like me for all the right reasons. I told him I was desperate to remain at Elstree and find work. He told me that Stanley Kubrick was just about to start going into production on a film called *The Shining*. With Malcolm's help I immediately applied to work on the film as a runner. Armed with a dazzling reference from Malcolm, I got the job. As I walked through the studio on my way home that evening, I could see the workers putting the final touches to the set where they had constructed the spooky Overlook Hotel that features throughout *The Shining*. I was in the film business. Two days later, I bumped into the producer as I was walking into the studio gates. 'I've got some bad news for you,' he said. 'Stanley Kubrick won't hire runners.' Apparently, I wasn't in the film business after all.

At this point, fate intervened. Though I didn't know it, Mum was convinced that my dream of working in the entertainment industry was a viable one. But not at Elstree. Aware that my contract there was coming to an end, she had sent a letter to EMI Music Publishing asking whether there were any vacancies in the postroom. EMI was known to us for other reasons, as my father ran their property division, and soon enough a man named Peter Schmidt wrote back to her saying that there was a vacancy available.

A week later, I went to meet the head of personnel at EMI. He had a star on his door, which kind of put me off a bit, but he was a nice guy and we immediately struck up a rapport. I was given an hour-and-a-half interview – in those days you were interviewed not just for your ability to sort mail, but for your overall career potential. The postroom was a place from which you could work your way up.

The following day, Peter phoned me. 'Simon,' he said, 'we have decided to offer you a job in the EMI mailroom.' I always knew that wearing jeans to an interview would one day pay off.

The very same day I was given the job at EMI, Stanley Kubrick happened to attend a charity dinner, where he was seated at the same table as Dad. Kubrick had already agreed to purchase our house, Abbots Mead, from Dad for rather a large sum of money, and as a result Dad and Stanley proceeded to celebrate the deal by consuming vast quantities of Scotch, during which time Dad skilfully persuaded Kubrick to reconsider giving me a job as a runner on *The Shining*. Dad was pretty good – on Scotch. Now I had two job offers on the same day.

By the following morning, I was totally confused. I had been happy working in the film business and learned a lot during my three months at Elstree. And up to that point, I hadn't once considered a career in the music industry. Plus, there was the Kubrick problem; Dad felt that we would be letting down the director if we didn't accept his generous offer. So we compromised: I decided to wake up the following morning, go to Elstree and meet up with my potential boss on *The Shining* to see if that would help influence my decision.

As I entered the studio gates, I noticed a crowd of about 30 men milling about, most of whom were in their forties or fifties. I was curious to know what they were waiting for so early in the morning, and I asked a guy at the end of the line. 'What are we queuing for?'

He said, gaping at me. 'For work, that's what we're queuing for, mate.'

Suddenly it dawned on me. Jobs here were really scarce,

and if you were lucky enough to get one, it wasn't necessarily a job for life. If this was the state of the British film business, I thought, well, then, bring on the music.

As soon as I got home, I phoned EMI and asked when I could start work. Lucky me. Lucky music business.

The postroom at EMI was a tiny basement office with high ceilings and bars on the windows. Though I was supposed to learn to deliver the mail, from my first day on the job I began planning and scheming my way to the top of the business. I thought it would be easy. It wasn't. In fact, it was downright tedious, but I never gave up. Determination and just a tiny bit of self-belief prevailed. This was my first audition, and I desperately wanted to make it through to the next round.

In many ways I was glad that I had started my career on the very bottom rung of the business. It was there that I learned how to deal with people – and not just those who couldn't sing. For me the biggest learning curve was what I learned about human nature. As a postroom boy, you get to meet people at all levels of the business. It was obvious to me that the people on the bottom rung looked up to those at the top, and the ones at the top invariably looked down on those at the bottom.

But my parents taught me that it doesn't matter how powerful or lowly your position is – you should still always treat people around you with manners and respect. Well, most of the time anyway.

O n my first day in the job, I was surprised to learn that postroom employees were not allowed to use the main entrance. Instead, we were told to go through the garages at the rear of the building. There I was greeted by this young guy wearing the biggest smile on his face I'd ever seen. 'Hi, I'm Colin Smith,' he said. 'You are my replacement.'

I said, 'So why are you so happy?'

'You haven't met the two guys you're working for yet,' he replied.

I followed Colin into the postroom. It was the worst room I have ever seen in my life. It was dark, damp, and airless.

With his smile broadening, Colin introduced me to Vic and Ron. Ron was adorable; he was about 65 and had the shakes but a kindly face. Sadly, he was only second in command. His boss was Vic, who turned out to be less affable. That's all I needed: a good cop and a bad cop.

Vic clearly wasn't happy about being in the postroom at such an advanced age. I felt that he also resented the fact that my dad managed EMI's property division and was on the board. I didn't give a damn – I had to do the job, not my dad. And while Vic thought that I was going to come in and use my dad's influence, the thought had never even crossed my mind. I suppose I was naive; I didn't realize at the time how much certain people would be wary of me for that reason.

You might think delivering mail is easy. It's not, particularly when you are struggling across Charing Cross Road pushing a mail trolley with one of the wheels about to come off. Nobody had told me that EMI had another office three blocks away, or that twice a day I would have to take my life in my hands by crossing four main roads with a load of mail.

As the new kid on the block, I expected a little bit of flack. But I wasn't prepared for the way that some of the other employees treated me simply because I was a post boy. It was unbelievable; it was as if they considered me the lowest form of life. But never once did I let their snide comments deter me from my main purpose. If anything, it just spurred me on.

For that first year and a half, I was on cloud nine because I had constant access to people who were very influential in the music industry. Even then, I didn't give a hoot what the etiquette was supposed to be. I would just barge into an office and ask for a better job. But after a while, it was apparent I was getting nowhere fast. I was still earning £25 a week and I felt it could take years to get out of the postroom. Furthermore, my division of EMI was a music publishing company – and I soon learned that the real sexy job in this business was to work for a record label.

One day I found out that there was a job opening at Ariola Records, which was part of BMG. It was what they called an independent and was considered a very cool label. Someone I knew tipped me off that the post boy had just left, and the next day I phoned up and said that I would be very interested in taking the job. I explained that I had always wanted to work for a record label and had put in a year at EMI. Essentially, I pleaded for an opportunity.

In the end, the man at Ariola said no, that I wasn't qualified enough. I was absolutely shattered. That night I went home and told my father that I wanted to leave the music industry. What made it even worse was the fact that my younger brother, Nicholas, had left college and got a job as an estate agent. He was earning £250 a week with a company car. Meanwhile, I was making £25 a week to deliver mail and be ridiculed.

I told Dad I'd had enough. I wasn't getting anywhere. I didn't think they were ever going to promote me. I wanted to leave and do what Nicholas was doing.

I could see Dad struggling to hold back a smirk. 'Are you absolutely sure about this?' he said.

'Yes,' I said. 'I'm positive. I've been there a year and a half now, and it looks like I'm never going to get out of the postroom.'

So out came Dad's book of jobs again – and you guessed

it, the book fell open at 'P' for Property. He picked up the phone and immediately got me a job at the snottiest firm of estate agents in the world.

Within a week, I had left the music business and was assigned to work for a miserable snobby guy who was about 35 years old. He had thick, ugly glasses and was losing his hair. He didn't like his job very much, and he didn't like me at all. We worked in the commercial division, so most of the job involved tallying sums on calculators, which I kept getting wrong. I opened his post, which I was good at, and made him tea.

After a week I went to my boss. 'Look,' I said. 'I would actually like to be doing something more than punching numbers into a calculator and making you tea.'

'OK,' he said, smugly, 'I've got just the job for you.'

'What is it?' I asked.

'Canvassing,' he replied.

Canvassing meant that I had to walk the entire length of Oxford Street (three miles), stand outside every shop, write down the name and phone number, and then move on to the next address. When I had finished, I had to cross the road and start doing all the shops down the opposite side of the road. And it was February – the snow was coming down, the wind was howling, and I had no coat. I don't recall how long this exercise took, but it was at least a week. Finally, I got back to the office with the list and handed it to my boss. He looked at it and said, 'I can't read your handwriting. Do it all again.'

I had never been so depressed in my life. It was the worst job I'd ever had. I had left the postroom hoping to improve my station; instead, I had sunk lower. Was this my future?

Fortunately, once again fate stepped in. Dad received a phone call from the managing director of EMI Publishing. He hadn't realized that I had left the company, and he told Dad that he wanted me to come back and work in the international division, which represented the writers and catalogues from American companies.

Dad immediately phoned me up at my office with the news. 'Will you take the job?' he said.

'Yes,' I said. 'When can I start?'

There was one last thing I needed to do before I left the estate agent's. I went straight to my boss's office with a huge grin on my face. 'So how are my job prospects going?' I asked him.

He looked up from his calculator and said, 'I don't really think you have the right attitude to be an estate agent.'

'I couldn't agree with you more' I replied. I shook his hand, packed my belongings and left.

* * *

That evening when I got home, I was on a high as I prepared myself for my re-entry into the music business. This time I was determined not to screw things up.

My high lasted until nine the following morning, when I walked into my new office at EMI. First, the job wasn't quite what I had expected. There were about ten people working in the department, and we were supposed to take songs and go around to record labels and see if we could get well-known artists to record the songs we represented.

Not yet an expert in office politics, I was unaware that there was a secretary in another division whose boss fancied her and had promised her the same job. This led to a rumour being circulated that I had only got the job because my dad was a pal of the managing director. Never mind that I had worked in the postroom for nearly two years. Nobody in the department would talk to me or even look at me. Welcome back, Simon.

I Don't Mean to Be Rude, But...
Punk Music Sucks

At the time I entered the music business, punk music was all the rage in Britain. When it all crumbled in the late seventies, I breathed a huge sigh of relief. I hated punk. It was sensationalistic, full of ugly people and no fun at all. Most of the band members couldn't sing a note or even play an instrument. At the height of the punk movement, there were a lot of people in the music business who had never been to see a punk band play live. One day a somewhat overenthusiastic (but pretty) music PR representative invited me to see one of the over-hyped bands who were about to be signed to a major label. Feeling a touch apprehensive, and clearly overdressed, I entered a sweaty basement club in Soho. When the band came onstage, they proceeded to jump up and down as if on pogo sticks. The audience spat beer at them and the band spat back. Great! I came out of the gig completely covered in spit – not one of my better nights out – and the band was crap. Punk was supposed to be anarchy, but I wasn't an angry young man. In a weird way it felt to me almost calculated. It was just a fad. By the time the Sex Pistols attempted to conquer America, the writing was already on the wall. At a Sex Pistols gig in Texas, Johnny Rotten walked out onstage wearing a T-shirt that said, 'You cowboys are all a bunch of fucking maggots.' The lights went out and the gig ended in a riot. It was the band's obituary. The only thing I loved from that era was the Sex Pistols' appearance on an evening show with Bill Grundy. It was the most cynical, brilliant piece of TV I have ever seen, and the Sex Pistols exploded after that. It was both funny and clever.

Dear Mr Cowell,

I watched with interest last Saturday's PopIdol. Your treatment of Mr Will Young was disgraceful. **HE IS THE POP IDOL**! I hope his father's shotgun is loaded and you get some 12 bore shot up your arse because you talk out of it.

He will win the competition and the whole of the country will know you don't know what you are talking about.

Miss G

3

Despite the ice-cold reception I received when I first arrived at my new job at EMI, I kept my head down and struggled on. Uncomfortable as it was being ostracized by most of the staff, office politics bored me. I saw these people as a waste of time and wasn't about to let them get the best of me. I was in, I was there, and I was going to make it.

At first, I gathered the whole catalogue, found a room with a tape player, and began to go through every single song. There were thousands of them. Some were country, some pop; some had been recorded by American artists but not covered by anyone in the UK. I noted the specific detail of every song and then drew up a 'hit list' of UK artists that I thought would work well with them. After six months, I had gained a better knowledge of the company's international song catalogue than anyone else in my department. As my confidence grew, I was ready to take my next step, which was to contact all the major record labels and start trying to sell our songs to their artists. The only obstacle I had to overcome was the A&R men.

Without question, A&R people were then the biggest arseholes in the music business. A&R stands for Artists and Repertoire. These are the guys who are responsible for signing artists, choosing the material for the artist, getting the right producer and generally keeping up with music trends – well, that was the theory. I soon discovered why I hated A&R people. My very first meeting was with a guy who was head of A&R at one of the major labels. He was well known in the business as being a little unhinged. I soon learned why. As I sat down opposite him in his office, he slowly began to take off his shoes and socks and then put his bare feet on the desk in front of my face as I talked.

It was an act of intimidation, pure and simple. Nowadays I would probably just laugh at him, but that day, on my first pitch to a major label, I was bemused. As my pitch came to a close, he just looked at me blankly. 'I don't think there's any decent material there for me,' he said. 'Come back when you have something hot.' I wasn't happy. I knew I had good material – but he was actually an idiot who didn't know what he was doing. The funny thing was, about a month later I had got about 15 or 20 songs placed with major artists on other labels and then he called me for an appointment. I didn't bother calling him back.

Despite the minor setbacks caused by crazed A&R men, I remained committed to learning my trade. But increasingly I was finding myself frustrated working at EMI. I was bored; I was very ambitious and already had my own ideas. I was also beginning to realize that this was a business you had to teach yourself – and that if I was going to do well, I would have to take risks.

So a year after I joined EMI I decided to quit my job and make a rather disastrous attempt to start my own music-publishing company. This ill-fated mission lasted about as long as an interview for one of Dad's bizarre jobs, but this time I learned a harsh lesson. Ellis Rich was my immediate boss at EMI. He had worked there for 18 years and was frustrated. We had begun to get on well, and this led him to suggest that we start our own publishing company. Naively I asked, 'What does that entail?'

'Making a lot of money,' he said. 'I think we can get funding, we can own the company and it can be our business.'

I was still very young, and I didn't really have much experience, but I knew Ellis had experience, and that made me feel more comfortable about the idea. He offered me a joint partnership. Deep down, I worried that we might be getting in over our heads. But I was tempted and flattered by Ellis's offer and his confidence in me. In the end, I chose to leave and started E&S Music.

Within a day of moving into our new offices in Soho, I realized I had made a big mistake. We didn't have the funding to do it properly: we couldn't get the business off the ground, and many of the fundamentals of running an independent company were foreign to us. After a week or so, I went back to see Ron White, who was the managing director at EMI. After overdoing the small talk, I finally summoned the courage to say, 'Look, Ron, I think I have made a big mistake. I admit I was wrong. Can I have my old job back?'

Ron just stared blankly at me. 'No, you can't,' he said. 'I trusted you, Simon, and I was going to nurture you. I was going to groom you for the top, but you've betrayed my trust. I can't have you back here.' I left the room feeling reprimanded, like I was back at school. But I knew he was right. Now I had no choice but to try and make it work with Ellis.

E&S Music was set up as an independent publishing company. We had signed a few writers, but the only way we were going to be able to survive was by getting representation in each country – and, more important, for each country to advance us money based on future earnings. Without these advances we were never going to survive the year. Our best shot was to go to America and try to drum up some business. It was my first trip to L.A., and the place seemed like paradise to me. On top of that, the prospects seemed good, at least at first – we had at least six or seven really positive meetings with publishing companies. Everyone, it seemed, wanted to work with us. On the way back on the plane, Ellis and I were both on a high and thought we had cracked America. But the joke was on us. We never heard from anyone we met in L.A. again. That's the thing about Los Angeles: it's a very difficult place to try and make it from the bottom up. It only works if you're dealing from a position of strength – a theory that I would test a little later.

About a year later, I decided I had to cut my losses. The business wasn't making money, and we were still struggling to get further financing. I was unhappy and wanted out, so I told Ellis I was quitting. He understood that I was ambitious and wanted to get out of music publishing. It was a bad period for me, but an experience that helped me focus on where I thought my future in the music business really was. Ellis went on to run his own very successful publishing company.

What I wanted to do was to make records. Hit records, preferably. But with my history in the business, it was unlikely that any record label would hire me as a producer or an A&R guy. What I did feel was that I had an instinctive understanding of what it took to generate a hit. I understood publishing, A&R and a bit about how to market records – but what my time at EMI had really shown me was that you first had to have great songs. I wanted to prove to myself that my instinct for finding hits would actually work. That's when I met up with an astute manager called Iain Burton.

Iain was about six years older than me. A former dancer, he had already made a lot of money from his management company supplying dancers for pop videos and TV. I had seen Iain a few times while I was at EMI, when he came in with artists he represented, and I had met him socially. That's how I heard he was looking to start a record label. While he had little knowledge of running a label, he was prepared to be an entrepreneur and take a risk. And let's face it: he was taking a huge gamble starting a record label with me. But like me, Iain was fascinated by the record industry and driven by the will to succeed, and I think that's why we hit it off. He recognized that I had something to prove. We decided to give it a go.

Being able to run things my way for the first time in the record business was a giant step. I wasn't daunted – I felt I was ready. Iain and I quickly struck a deal, and he agreed to pay me £65 a week. (One lesson I have learned over the years is never to over-negotiate your initial salaries. If things work out afterwards, the money will follow. Ask for too much at the beginning and you may not get the job.) One of the upsides to this new job was working out of Iain's offices on South Molton Street. In those days South Molton Street was like a catwalk. The street was lined with trendy clothes shops and cafés, and had quickly become home to London's top model agents. It was incredible.

At the beginning, we didn't even focus on music. Iain had watched Jane Fonda make a fortune from launching the first exercise video, and the global success of that endeavour had given birth to a lucrative market in aerobics videos. Everyone in Britain wanted to jump on the bandwagon, but Iain got there first and made a video with a British choreographer named Arlene Philips. Arlene was a friend and client of Iain's and one of the most successful choreographers in Britain. Just about every major recording artist in the world wanted her to work on their videos. She already had a profile from working on TV with a very successful dance act called Hot Gossip. The video sold hundreds of thousands of copies, and our new label, Fanfare Records, was born.

I was now running my own record label. This was a godsend, and it was also a problem. I didn't have a secretary, didn't have a postroom boy and didn't have any A&R men. Oh – and I didn't have any recording artists, either.

* * *

This was all about to change when I met a singer from Seattle named Sinitta. It was to be my first big break.

We met in a nightclub. Sinitta was cute, funny and had long dark hair that went almost to her waist. I gave her some cheesy line about running a record label, and she said, 'That's cool – I'm a singer. Why don't you make a record with me? Let's meet up and talk about it.' Of course, I didn't want to meet up to talk business. I wanted to take her out.

The following day, she turned up at my office and played me some demo tapes she had made. I was shocked to discover that she had a great pop voice. And as I already knew from the nightclub, she could dance. (Her mother, I would find out later, was Miquel Brown, who had a number of hits in the early eighties, including 'So Many Men, So Little Time'.) I agreed to sign her up as an artist. It was the least I could do. Sinitta became my first signing, but at the time I had absolutely no idea what I was going to do with her.

This was a rich period of learning for me; in the span of 12 months I would have to learn to single-handedly master everything: signing artists, making records, commissioning videos and selling records to the retailers, not to mention the mind-numbingly dull issues like managing stock control. With the success of the exercise video Iain had made a lot of money and he was now willing to let me have free rein. What I wanted to do was build a successful record label, and I was determined to succeed at all costs.

I met a well-known songwriter and asked him to try and come up with some suitable tracks. He eventually came back with a song called 'So Macho'. It was perfect for Sinitta, and the moment I heard it I knew it was going to be a huge hit. I drove straight over to Sinitta's apartment to play it to her. She loved it, and we were both really excited. But while I was there, Iain Burton telephoned me. 'Simon,' he said, 'I need to tell you something.' I could tell by his voice he wasn't planning to raise my salary, and there was an uncomfortable pause. 'Look,' he said, 'I have to close down the record label.' I was stunned and demanded to know why. 'I'm putting all my money into a new project, so I need to close down the label,' he said. 'I don't really like the record business. So I'm sorry – it's over.' We hadn't even started!

Now my mind was racing. 'Wait,' I said. 'Iain, listen. I think we've got a hit record here with Sinitta, and I'm begging you, please don't close this label down. Just give me some money and I'll make this record a hit.' I eventually convinced him to give me £5,000 to cover everything, including the video. I had a feeling the video wasn't going to be 'Thriller'.

* * *

The pressure turned out to be a blessing in disguise. The stakes were high, and I was forced to work with a tiny budget and rely on sheer drive and enthusiasm to try to create a hit. I had no idea if it would work, but I knew that if I blew it, I wouldn't even be a one-hit wonder. I made a video for £2,000 – and it looked like a £1,500 video. Then I hired a record plugger, but I told him I would pay him only if he got results. I was desperate. When we finally put the record out, it entered the UK charts at around number 40 and then stalled. But there was actually some momentum on the sales front – the sales just kept chugging along. So I released it a second time – and nothing. The third time was the charm. Within a few months we had sold just under 900,000 copies and 'So Macho' had reached number two in the charts. In the end, we had done the whole thing for just £5,000 and made close to £1 million profit. More importantly, I had my first hit single. But even better Iain decided that he wanted to reinvest in the record label.

With my job and the future of the label now secure, I pondered what to do next. I honestly believed that Sinitta had tremendous potential beyond this first hit. By this time she had a loyal fan base and had built up a huge following. It was just a question of finding the right song for a follow-up single.

It was at this critical stage in my career that I began to

understand the true value of using the best producers and writers. I went on to learn that without a committed hit writing and production team behind you it is almost impossible to successfully launch a pop star who doesn't write their own material. There was a buzz at the time about three new record producer/writers called Stock, Aitken & Waterman. Pete Waterman was the guy who had put the three of them together. A former gravedigger, he had been a successful club DJ before becoming one of Britain's most accomplished record producers and songwriters. He would go on to have more than 30 No. 1 hits and 70 top-20 records during the eighties and nineties. They owned pop music. Pete has claimed he has sold an astonishing 500 million singles in his career. Years later he would sit alongside me as a judge on *Pop Idol*. Today he is one of my best friends in the music industry.

Back then, however, Pete was just starting out. His first real hit was by a singer named Hazel Dean. The record went to number three, and when I heard it I knew instantly that whoever had written and produced it were geniuses. I was right.

I was desperate to get Stock, Aitken & Waterman to write a song for Sinitta – I knew I had one shot to take her to the next level, and I couldn't afford anything less than a worldwide hit single. Since I have never been shy about opening my mouth, I phoned up Pete Waterman and said, 'We haven't spoken before. My name's Simon Cowell. I look after a singer named Sinitta, and I would like to come and talk to you about working with us.' He agreed to meet with me.

I arrived at his studio, which in those days consisted of crumbling plaster walls and discarded plastic coffee cups all over the floor. Abbey Road it wasn't. We had to sit on wooden crates. At the time, Pete was in his mid-forties, with thinning grey hair. He was really full of himself. It was a bit like looking in the mirror – apart from the hair.

'I have a hunch that you guys are going to be huge,' I began.

'So do I,' he said.

'Well, I want to hire you to produce a follow-up for Sinitta.'

Pete smiled and said, 'I'm too busy.'

'On what?' I asked him, looking around at this dump of a recording studio.

Pete just winked and said, 'You'll see.'

I didn't really know why, but I was convinced that Pete was the man who could provide the next hit for Sinitta, and more. I didn't want to let the moment pass, so I tried another angle. 'If I find the right song, will you produce it for us?' I asked him.

Pete began to laugh. 'You don't take no for an answer, do you?'

At that point he more or less threw me out of the studio, saying that if I sent him some songs he would give me his opinion, that's all – if he had the time.

Weeks later, Pete's career exploded. Stock, Aitken & Waterman were a phenomenon and had the music industry eating out of its hand. With hits for artists including Donna Summer, Dead or Alive, Bananarama, Kylie Minogue and Rick Astley, Stock, Aitken & Waterman became the most successful writing and production team in history. There was just one problem – where was my Sinitta hit?

I was sharp enough to know that Pete could become my mentor. He had knowledge of the industry and a cultural savvy that I craved, and I wanted to learn what it took to get to his level. Every day that I could get away from the office, I showed up at Pete's studio and followed his every move. I was still looking for that elusive hit for Sinitta, and I knew that he was the one to help. He was arrogant, conceited and rude – and a genius. My kind of guy.

In those days, Pete's studio was total chaos. People were constantly coming and going, and artists were in the studio recording night and day. No one thought it odd that I would drift in from time to time. But after a few months of being there, Pete pulled me to one side. 'Simon,' he said, 'am I mistaken in thinking that you've turned up every day for the past few months? What exactly are you doing here?'

'Seeing how you work,' I said. 'Learning the business.'

'Well, I'm not going to pay you,' he warned.

'I don't want you to pay me,' I said.

Now he was getting irritated. 'Then what the fuck do you want?'

'Just to follow you around,' I said. And that's what I did. When I had the opportunity, I would go into the studio and watch the way Pete handled the engineers and producers during a recording. I began to learn all about what it takes to produce a hit. A song can be mind-blowing, but it's the production and the final mix that determine how successful the record will be.

Years later, Pete would tell me about the first time he saw me in the studio with Westlife, my first bona fide breakout success. He noticed the way I expressed myself to the engineers, how I told them what I wanted from the final mix, and he said it was precisely the same way that he worked in the studio. When I first began shadowing Pete, I already knew what I wanted to hear from the final mix of a song, but I had to learn how to tell the engineers and producers what I wanted. That, in essence, is what I learned from Pete Waterman: the language and the know-how. It was also Pete who told me that there is only one key area of pop music: the song.

Ironically, after all that education, I was still looking for that elusive second song for Sinitta, and I still believed Pete was the only person who could help. In the meantime, Sinitta had been making a good living touring the clubs and doing public appearances around the country. But at this point she was still my only artist. I had a responsibility to make her successful. If I could take her to the next level, the label would also start to have credibility. So I continued to make a nuisance of myself and badger Pete to write a song at every opportunity. Whenever I did, he would just frown and say, 'I'm too busy to write songs. You find me the right track and I'll produce it for you.' Each time I thought I had found a hit song, I would play it and he would shout over it, 'Crap, crap, crap ... you don't know what you're talking about. Come back to me when you've got something worth listening to.' His ranting only made me more determined to succeed. (I'm often asked if I can take criticism, and I always think back to these days, when the tough feedback of someone who knew more than me helped me so much more than fake praise.)

One day I read an article in the newspaper about the new trend of celebrities stepping out with younger guys. Toyboys, they were called. So I telephoned Pete and said, 'I have a great title for a song, "Toyboy". I'm sure it will work, Pete, just write the song.' He said grudgingly, 'Yeah, you're right. It is a good title. I could write a song in about five minutes.'

'OK, do it,' I challenged him.

'No!' he shouted. 'I'm too bloody busy.' He slammed down the phone. I could feel Sinitta breathing down my neck.

Three months later Pete called me, sounding really excited. 'Simon, get down to the studio now. I've got your hit!'

'What hit?' I asked.

'"Toyboy", mate. I've written it.'

I will never forget that moment. Even then, I knew it was going to change my life. I raced down to Pete's studio. I could barely breathe. And the second he put it on, I knew it was going to be a huge hit. We brought Sinitta straight into the studio that day and started recording. With Pete's help, 'Toyboy' went on to be an even bigger hit for Sinitta than 'So Macho'. It sold millions all over the world, and it finally helped to get my label taken seriously. There was still a long way to go.

I Don't Mean to Be Rude, But...
Michael Jackson Is a Spoiled Brat

Without a doubt, Michael Jackson made some of the best pop records of all time. If you were to list the 50 best pop songs in history, you would have many Michael Jackson songs on that list: 'Billie Jean', 'Thriller', 'Black or White'. He was a genius. But the last record he released, Invincible, *was one of the weakest efforts I had ever heard. He went on television and blamed Sony for everything. He said that they weren't behind him, that they were racist; he launched a ridiculous attack against Tommy Mottola the boss of Sony. The simple truth, as anyone who heard the record knows, is that the new record was crap. The songs were weak: he'd lost his spark, his individuality, his edge. The notion that the record company somehow sabotaged him is just idiotic: I'm sure people actually lost their jobs when the record performed badly. The weirdness in his life hasn't helped matters, of course, because it has made it so that he can't be taken seriously. I felt quite bad for him after that documentary with Martin Bashir. But he's the equivalent of a Victorian freak show. I'd watch anything on him; it's a train wreck. But it doesn't help him return to being a serious pop artist. If I were entrusted with fixing his career, I would probably tell him to camp outside Quincy Jones's house. Their partnership worked for him. I don't know why he abandoned it. The other producers just failed to understand that you can't make him sound like everybody else. He's not everybody else. He's Michael Jackson.*

Dear Nasty Pop Idol judge,

What gives you the right to criticise singers.
What would you say to Cliff Richards if he
came on your show? "Sorry Mr Richards you
are too old."

I have just purchased a new television set
complete with remote control which fortunately
comes with a 'mute' button. This comes in
particulary handy when you are summing up
on the show.

Yours sincerely

Mrs Y (aged 64)

Fanfare Records and Sinitta continued to have a string of hits throughout the 1980s. We began to break her as an artist in other parts of the world, most notably Japan, and in Britain she became one of the biggest-selling pop artists; her earning potential was now phenomenal. The downside was that our relationship deteriorated. We had started to date in 1985 but it was impossible to date her and be her record label, and we eventually agreed it would be just business from now on.

As it turns out, that didn't hurt our friendship one bit. I'm very lucky, because in the main most of the relationships I've had have been brilliant both during and after they have finished. I can't really think of anybody who I've dated who I hate or who hates me. In fact, some of my ex-girlfriends remain my best friends to this day, three in particular.

Sinitta was the first test case for this. When we were dating and working together, we used to argue like mad, and every time we had an argument and it looked like we'd broken it off, she sent me a letter that started with 'Dear Simon, back to business'. And I would only ever read the opening line and the final line, because I couldn't bear to read the bits in the middle. I knew it was just going to be terrible. Amazingly, though, once the relationship drifted away, we managed to carry on working together for a number of years and she became in some ways the unofficial daughter of the Cowell family. Mum and Dad were always very fond of her; in fact, when we were dating she lived at my parents' house with me for a while.

When she (finally) got married, which happened only recently, she was living in my house at Holland Park at the time. I knew that things were getting serious with her and her boyfriend, and I hoped that the two of them would get married because I wanted her to find somebody who genuinely loved her. Sinitta is wonderful, but she's a handful too, and she has always needed someone to be strong with her as well. At any rate, she was living there as my houseguest, and she and Andy went away, and then the next thing I knew, she was telling me that she was going to be married. I thought she was joking, but she muttered some details. We were invited to the reception, not the wedding, so we all turned up to one of our favourite restaurants, about 100 of us, and when we got there, they both looked fabulous, very, very happy, and then Andy stood up and said, 'We want to show you a film.' It turned out that they had been married a week before in Las Vegas. They got married in a bloody helicopter. She has found stability with someone who loves her, and in the end that's what you want for all your exes. She will always be one of my best friends for the rest of my life, and she helped make me aware of an important fact: just because a woman isn't your girlfriend, that doesn't mean she can't stay in your life.

By the time Sinitta's career took off, I had accomplished two things: I had broken an artist worldwide and I had now become good friends with one of the most successful producers in the business. And more importantly, I had learned things from Pete that I would never have learned at a major label. The day I met Pete Waterman was easily the most important day of my career.

I Don't Mean to Be Rude, But...
Why Can't Your Ex-girlfriend Be Your Best Friend?

Another one of my ex-girlfriends who I probably see more of than anybody else in my life is Jackie St Clare. Jackie and I dated for three months before I met Sinitta. The funny story about Jackie was that I first met her in a bar in the West End called Mortons when I was 24 years old. I was busy chatting some girl up who was sitting behind me and in walked Jackie. I suddenly forgot all about the girl I was talking to and fixated on Jackie. I thought she was one of the most beautiful girls I'd ever seen in my life, and I didn't have the guts to go up and speak to her, so I had a friend of mine who was sitting with me go and talk to her, figuring that at least I'd get an introduction. He went over there, and five minutes later, he was back, saying she wasn't interested in him but that she did want to meet me. I introduced myself and ended up falling for her big time. We were about the same age, but I was relatively naive and she was very worldly. I knew at once that I was out of my depth. From the start, I knew that I'd seen her somewhere before, but I couldn't quite put my finger on it.

Over the course of the first week, I realized where I'd seen her: she was Miss Nude UK and I'd seen her in Mayfair or something. So now I had a date with Miss Nude UK. If that wasn't intimidating enough, the following week, when we went on a date, Jackie brought her portfolio with her, and it was full of glamour shots. I was really awkward, and I kept making inane remarks about the beach in the background, or the sunset. At the time I had no money at all – nothing – and I knew this was a girl who wasn't going to be satisfied with McDonald's or KFC. I

went to see my dad, and asked him if I could go on his member-
ship to 'Rags', which was a private members club in Mayfair. We
had a great dinner, I signed for it and she was suitably
impressed. Then the dating began. To be honest, while I liked her
tremendously, and more and more as we went on, I knew that I
would never hold on to her. Maybe it was a lack of confidence, or
a lack of money, but here was a girl who could have had any man
in London. What was she doing with me? One afternoon I
phoned her to see if we were going out that night and she said no.
I said well what about tomorrow? No. Following day? 'Look,
Simon,' she said, 'we're never going out again.' Ah. I put the
phone down. I was really upset, but there was nothing I could do
about it. About six weeks later the phone rang. It was my birthday and it was Jackie. 'Hi,' she said, as if nothing had happened.
'Happy Birthday. What are you doing to celebrate?' I told her
that a group of us were going to Rags, and she invited herself
along. I pretended that I didn't think it was a good idea, but I
was thrilled. She turned up and flirted with every single guy
there except me. She ignored me all night long except for the last
minute of the party, when she invited me to come back to her flat.
I spent the night there – or most of the night, actually. At about
three in the morning she threw me out. I was devastated. About
three months after that Jackie and I had dinner, and I realized
that I was no longer worried about the relationship. I liked her
as a friend, and we have been inseparable for 20 years. Even to

this day, she'll turn up at my place at nine thirty in the morn-
ing, prepare breakfast with me, come upstairs and have break-
fast in bed (I'm in the bed, she's on the bed). She comes on holi-
days with me most years. We are inseparable, like Siamese twins.
I can't imagine Jackie not being in my life. It would be like
cutting off an arm.

    Mandy Perryment is another one of my close girlfriends.
When I first met Mandy she was dating my younger brother
Nicholas (being similar in age, Nicholas and I have always
been competitive over girls). But we didn't start dating for 15
more years. We had always been very, very close, but one day,
over the phone, when she was in Los Angeles and I was in
London, we just decided to have an affair. We arranged to meet
in Miami and we ended up having an amazing relationship
for a few months. It kind of fizzled out, but it wasn't even
awkward and it didn't cause any problems once we weren't
going out any longer. I don't talk to Mandy as much as I talk to
Jackie, but there's never any awkwardness if we haven't spoken
for two or three months. She's one of the best friends I have.

In the British music business there has always been great
importance placed on the idea of integrity and credibility.
Punk was seen as having 'street cred', which meant that the
artists weren't artificially constructed by a record company
but represented something real from the clubs and the

neighbourhoods that would be recognized as legitimate by record buyers. I still think punk was a low point. The first wave of New Romantics – bands like ABC, Duran Duran, and so forth, which picked up on the style and flair of seventies bands like Roxy Music and David Bowie – fell into the same category, before other artists jumped onto the bandwagon. In the mid-eighties, the ultimate in 'non-cred' was to be associated with the country's biggest hitmakers, Stock, Aitken & Waterman. Their songs were simply too commercial for some tastes. Not for me. If I want art, I'll buy it. For me the decision was clear-cut. Pop was what I liked and understood. Pop for me would always be the future.

By 1985 my partner, Iain Burton, was looking to expand his business. He had identified a gap in the electronics market, of all things, and developed a number of handheld gadgets, including a currency calculator, which he marketed throughout Europe. For Iain our future lay in diversification; I, however, wanted to keep developing a successful record label. The music industry press at the time saw the growth of independent labels like Fanfare as a healthy alternative to the major labels.

The major difficulty in being a small label is ensuring proper distribution for your records. As a result, Fanfare had struck up a distribution deal with one of the major record labels, BMG.

I soon learned that certain people at BMG had been charting my course and were looking to hire me to come and work there, and in 1989 I was offered the chance to join BMG Records as an A&R consultant. This was my biggest career break so far. The consultancy meant I would remain independent, and the company promised me free rein on whatever I wanted to do, with one proviso: I had to sell a minimum number of records in the first year if I wanted my option taken up.

In short, being an A&R consultant meant I had to identify new talent, find new songs, and break as many records as possible. Given the financial security and marketing budget that came with a major label like BMG, it wasn't a hard decision to make.

I left Fanfare Records – and, I should say, Iain and I did not part company amicably. I was, however, grateful for the help that he had given me. Iain was the best salesman I have ever met and everything he did reaffirmed my belief that you should never take 'No' for an answer.

From the outset I had talks with my bosses at BMG during which I set out my vision. My vision, in short, was television. In 1981, MTV had changed the face of the music industry entirely, and very quickly video became king. In those days, without a really hot video, it was virtually impossible to break a new artist and have a hit record.

In the early days of MTV, music videos had small budgets and production values to match – take my Sinitta video as an example – but kids were hooked, and then more imaginative, elaborate and expensive videos like Peter Gabriel's 'Sledgehammer' upped the ante. Very soon record companies were spending more and more money to make their videos slicker and more stylish. The competition for chart position depended on these television spots. Michael Jackson topped everyone by spending $4 million on his 'Thriller' video, which helped make the album of the same name the greatest seller of all time. I still think 'Thriller' remains the best pop video ever made. Jackson treated the whole thing as you would a movie. He hired John Landis to direct it, after seeing his hit film *An American Werewolf in London*. He even made sure he got the same make-up artists and special-effects specialists to work on the video. He just got it right.

MTV was already a media force, so I wasn't the only one to have the bright idea. But I was the only one to have the brightest version of it. For me, it wasn't just about videos but the entire medium of television. I felt that major record companies had failed to understand the importance of TV as a medium in breaking artists or records. Trying to get radio play as a new artist is a nightmare. Television has a huge captive audience and also the ability to create something unique for an artist, a vision, an image and emotion – the most important factor in selling pop music.

Around that time, I cut a deal that would change my life. I read in a newspaper that the World Wrestling Federation (WWF) had come over to tour Britain and had sold out Wembley Stadium in 27 minutes. I knew that there were few music artists who could sell out an 80,000-seat venue in that amount of time. So I phoned up the boss at WWF, Vince McMahon, and said, 'Have you ever thought about making an album with your wrestlers?'

As luck would have it, one of McMahon's managers was in town the next day and we had a breakfast meeting. I persuaded him that the deal was a good idea, and at my insistence Pete Waterman and Mike Stock wrote and produced the album. This would be the first record I would release to test this theory of mine. Could I sell albums without any radio play at all and rely on the word of mouth buzz created by television? The single went to No. 3 in the charts and the album went on to sell more than 1.5 million copies throughout Europe. Even though I knew at the time that The Undertaker and Randy Savage certainly weren't what you'd call career artists, the experience proved I was correct in my thinking. This, I realized, was an area within the industry that I could capitalize on, and possibly even own.

To say that I faced resistance from within the music business was an understatement. At that point, I was at Arista Records, which was one of the labels under the BMG umbrella, and people weren't necessarily thrilled with the idea of signing up television characters. Before the WWF record came out, in fact, one senior executive at the label actually got down on his knees and begged me not to do the deal with the wrestlers. Other people at the label wanted credibility. I wanted hits, and I couldn't have cared less about credibility. Still, the constant negativity got to me. I went through a stage when I had records that were succeeding but never quite made it into the Top Ten, and I began to have grave doubts about my course. When you're in an environment like that, you need supportive people around you, and I didn't have many.

Still, I knew in my heart that I was right. In fact, after the WWF record came out, I went through a phase where I was somewhat fanatical about making records with television characters and personalities. I set my sights on Zig and Zag, who were puppets on Channel 4's TV show *The Big Breakfast*. They were absolutely massive at the time and everyone in Britain was talking about them. I also signed the Power Rangers, who were the biggest toy phenomenon in history. Those were the days when singles could sell two million copies, and I was very enthusiastic about these two acts. I remember sitting down with my assistant at the time and telling her that if those two records didn't take off, I was going to leave the business for a year. If my instincts about them were wrong, then my entire perspective on the industry was off, and something would have to change.

That was the consensus, certainly. I remember a board meeting in which my assistant and I presented our latest signings to the record label heads. We went through an endless series of flip charts, talked about domestic signings and other boring matters. Then I raised my hand and announced that I had two major signings: Zig and Zag and the Power Rangers. There were sneers and muffled laughter around the room. One of the directors asked me if they could hear the records before we went any further. 'With respect,' I said, 'if you've got a record by Zig and Zag or the Power Rangers, you can make a calculated guess that they're going to sell a lot of copies.'

'Well, I refuse to do anything until I hear the records,' one of them said.

I went to my office and brought back the rough demo I had done with Zig and Zag – it was just a drum track with their sample vocals over the top. I put it on in the meeting, and after 15 seconds the director turned off the machine and drew a zero on the flip chart – they didn't think the record had a chance. At that point I got up, shook hands with everybody around the table, and made an announcement. 'Just to let you know,' I said, 'this will be the last time you ever see me again, because I'm walking out of here.'

I went straight to the office of John Preston, the chairman of BMG, and told him that he needed to move me to another label or lose me entirely. He called up RCA, another label in the BMG family, and just like that I was transferred. Jeremy Marsh was the managing director and Hugh Goldsmith was head of marketing. They were great fun and very supportive, and to this day they remain two of my best friends. Monday morning, at RCA, I brought up the Power Rangers deal, and they were instantly enthusiastic. I flew to L.A., came back with the deal, and we put both singles out. Of all the records I have ever put out in my life, these were the most pivotal. I really felt that my instincts were right, and if the records hadn't worked it would have proved to me – and the rest of the industry – that I had lost my touch.

By this time, I had begun to think very differently from most people in the music business. Most of my colleagues were obsessed with signing the next coolest rock or alternative band, and I was considered by many to be a laughing stock, a freak. 'You're signing wrestlers, puppets, the fucking Power Rangers!' one senior executive screamed at me once. 'What kind of future do you have?' Well, that was the point – I felt that I was latching on to something unique that could potentially grow into a fantastic business. I always used to say to people during this period, 'Laugh all you want. This is my target practice.' In other words, I was still learning the business. The process of having one-off hit records taught me an enormous amount about understanding trends in the marketplace. And I knew even then that the link between television and music would be even more important in years to come.

One guy at RCA, Mike McCormack, gave me some great advice at that time. 'Simon,' he said, 'you're like Gary Lineker. Wait by the goal, wait for the ball and then nod it in the goal.' In other words, be patient and wait for the right thing to come your way. It was good advice.

Fortunately, I hadn't lost my touch at all. Both the Zig and Zag and Power Rangers tracks were Top 3 singles, and between the two of them RCA sold one-and-a-half million copies. We then sold over a million Power Rangers albums around the world off the back of that one single. It was a huge victory for me, especially given the reluctance of some of the people at Arista. Would these records touch people the way John Lennon's 'Imagine' had? No. But they still found an enormous audience. And they restored my confidence. The fact that I now had somebody who believed in me and the fact that I had been right meant everything to me. Everyone needs that kind of confidence restorer at some point in their career. I did decide, however, that it would be nice to have some hits with humans, rather than robots or aliens.

Not every television property was a sure thing. Through the music community, I heard that the comedian Eddie Murphy was looking to make an album – and not a comedy album, either, but a pop music album. After making contact through his managers, I flew to the United States to have a meeting with him at his house outside New York. Thinking that he was going to play me some tracks on his personal stereo, I was a little surprised to be taken down to the basement, where he had his own state-of-the-art recording studio. An entourage, 15-strong, surrounded Eddie. It was quite obvious to me that a lot of those guys were making a good living from the Eddie Murphy Music Project. And it was also obvious why: when it came to music, Eddie had a sense-of-humour bypass. He took his new music career very seriously – very, very seriously! I asked to hear some of the songs he was thinking of recording, which of course he had written himself. After song 12, I was losing the will to live. I had run out of fake compliments. I thought every recording was ghastly. Various yes-men were busy nodding their heads and smiling like a gospel choir. I turned to Eddie and whispered in his ear, 'Is it at all possible that we could have a word in private?' He could see by my face I was serious, and he told the 'choir' to leave the studio. I then explained in no uncertain terms that the songs were not up to standard.

'What's wrong with them?' he asked.

'Eddie,' I replied, 'they're crap. If you really want to break into pop music, then I suggest you come to the UK and work with some of our producers.' I actually believed that we could make it work; Bruce Willis had recently released an album that had sold nearly a million copies in the UK.

A week later, I got a call from his manager giving me the details of his travelling party. It read like a scene from *Coming to America*. The entourage included about 30 hangers-on. I calculated that it would cost me close to £500,000 to fly him in to record three or four songs. That was unacceptable. I was on the phone to Eddie straightaway.

'Why do you need all these people?' I asked him.

'Well, that's how we normally travel,' he said.

'OK,' I said, 'the deal's off.' I never spoke to him again. I did hear that he went on to enjoy some success in films.

Another television star that I worked with during my early days at BMG Records was David Hasselhof. At that time, David was not just a television personality. He had been very successful in Germany, selling millions of records, and he was desperate to break into the UK market. I got a call from one of the top executives at BMG in New York who told me that David was one of the company's biggest-selling artists in Germany, and that he really wanted a hit in the UK. I was basically told, 'Get him a hit.' While David's image in England was certainly that of a big star, mainly due to the success of *Baywatch*, I had severe doubts that anyone would take him seriously as a singer.

I arranged for a very credible journalist to meet David in London, and we agreed that the interview would focus on his singing career, and the success he had had in Germany. We met David at his hotel, where he was staying with his sidekick, a guy named Buddy. We sat down at the table, and almost immediately David began to tell a story about how he had just returned from a trip to Africa. 'I had this amazing experience while I was there,' he said. 'I held up my son to the dawn. I can honestly say I have truly discovered the importance of life.' Everyone around the table remained silent. I found it excruciating. Then, to my horror, David looked like he was going to cry. The journalist couldn't believe her luck. I had to use every inch of my considerable charm to persuade the reporter not to write anything about this very strange meeting. It wasn't the best of starts, but worse was to follow.

I approached Pete Waterman to see if he would work with David and produce some songs. Initially, he said yes, he would be delighted. But several weeks later, after a number of meetings with David, Pete suddenly called, saying he couldn't work with him any more. 'He's just too demanding,' he said. 'It's too much work.'

I was horrified. 'Pete,' I pleaded, 'will you reconsider? He's really excited about working with you.'

'Too bad, mate,' Pete said. 'I'm not doing it.'

Two hours later, I got a call from David. 'When do we start recording?' he asked.

'Well, actually we're not,' I said. 'Pete doesn't feel that he can work with you.'

'What do you mean he can't work with me?' David demanded. 'Doesn't he like my singing?'

'He didn't mention your singing,' I told him.

'Right,' he said. 'Meet me in one hour at the hotel; I'll be in the restaurant.' And he slammed down the phone.

When I arrived at the hotel, there were six people sitting with him around a table and the restaurant was packed. As I walked towards them, expecting a big shouting match, I saw that David had a horrible grin on his face. He pulled out a boom box. 'So I'm not good enough to work with Pete Waterman, am I?' he said, leering at me. Then he pressed Play; on came the backing track to Jackie Wilson's 'Your Love Is Lifting Me Higher', which he proceeded to sing in my face in front of the whole restaurant. Halfway through the song the maître d appeared. 'If you want to sing in your suite, Mr Hasselhof, I can arrange it – but we don't allow it in the dining room.' I gave that guy the biggest tip of his career.

In the end we hired a new production and writing team, put David in the studio, and finally gave him a hit record in the UK. Unfortunately, success didn't improve his dress sense. It fell to me to persuade him not to wear an electric-blue suit while appearing on *Top of the Pops*. Street cred? I don't think so.

At my final meeting with him, I couldn't resist having the last word. He was in his hotel suite surrounded by his team of people. 'David,' I said, 'the problem with you is that you are incredibly precious.'

A horrible silence followed, and his entourage looked on in total disbelief. David looked at me and whispered, 'Did you just call me precious, Simon?'

I nodded grimly.

'You're absolutely right, Simon!' he shouted. 'I am precious.' He seemed pleased about this. I always thought David was hysterically funny, though I can't say that his comedy was always intentional. Working with people like him – or Eddie Murphy, for that matter – was quite an education. I grew accustomed to dealing with people who were certain that they had futures as pop stars, even if much of the available evidence suggested the exact opposite. Hmmmm.

After the WWF, after Zig and Zag, and after the Power Rangers, I was doing well financially, but not as well as others in the business. I was making a small fortune, but not a large one. And I was, as always, very competitive. I wanted to be the top dog within RCA, and I wasn't happy that other A&R men were having bigger hits than I was. In fact, it made me very depressed. I could talk about teamwork, and the good of the company, and all the other clichés, but why bother? The idea of rooting for your fellow A&R men has always seemed like a big lie to me. I'm as competitive with somebody who works for my company as I am with somebody who works for another label, and in a way it makes it worse. In fact, if a fellow A&R man was happy for my success, I would find that very odd.

I was still having quite a lot of chart success at this time. I signed Sonia (sweet) and Curiosity Killed The Cat (difficult). And then I hit the jackpot! There was a girl working for our sales division at the time, a very bright girl named Denise Beighton, and she had an uncanny ability to spot a hit record. She just knew. One morning, she walked into my office and said something strange. 'By the way,' she said, 'we're getting a ton of phone calls from every retailer in

England asking if we're responsible for anything by Robson and Jerome.' Interestingly, my brother Nicholas had called me the previous night about Robson and Jerome and I didn't take any notice. Denise explained they were actors in the TV series *Soldier Soldier*. 'Last night they sang a version of "Unchained Melody", and the reaction has been amazing,' she said. I called the television producer; she said that their office had also been besieged by calls. And then I called up about ten record stores across England – they, too, were getting hundreds of inquiries. I called the producer right back and asked for an introduction to Robson and Jerome, only to be told that they weren't interested. I called their agents and reached the same dead end. It was very frustrating, but I kept on. It was becoming clear that I needed to talk to them and try to persuade them to release the single, so I continued to try and get in contact with them. A few weeks later, just before I was going to go on holiday, I received a phone call from someone representing Robson Green. He told me that Robson was going to take legal action if I continued to harass him; at this point, I was sending letters, faxes, hand-delivered notes, everything. No response. I went on holiday, but after a few days I couldn't stand it any longer and flew back to the UK. When I got back, I kept calling, once a day, twice a day, ten times a day. I just went mental. I wouldn't give up. Eventually, the phone rang and it was Robson Green. 'Why are you harassing me and my family?' he screamed.

'Why won't you talk to me?' I said.

'Because I'm not interested,' he said.

'Why?' I asked.

'Because I don't want to appear on *Top of the Pops.*'

That's when I made my offer. 'Listen,' I said. 'Just for one second. If you go in and cut this record for me, I'll give you and Jerome £50,000 each. Even if I don't put the record out, I'll pay you. Think about it: two hours' work, £50,000 at worst. And if you like it and you're willing to talk, then we'll talk about a deal.'

'Are you prepared to put that in writing?' he said. I couldn't have agreed fast enough. I went to his agent's office immediately.

On the way over, I realized that I had no idea what he looked like. I hadn't seen a single episode of the show even once. I walked into the office and blurted out, 'Simon here.' Thankfully, Robson waved back. He was insistent on talking about his television character. For half an hour, I lied through my teeth about my admiration for the show, and how important and worthwhile it was. Finally, he asked if I was serious about the deal. I said I was, and I gave him a letter there and then.

I set up the recording date with Pete Waterman's

production partners, Mike Stock and Matt Aitken, and they started cutting the record. When I went down to the studio for a check-in, I knew they were hooked. Robson and Jerome were sitting in the recording booth listening to the record, and they were both as excited as children. Robson looked at me with mock anger. 'You bastard,' he said. 'You knew this would happen. We just love the record.'

They agreed to make a single, but on one condition: They didn't want to appear on *Top of the Pops*. I agreed. We had a deal.

On the way home, I played the Righteous Brothers original of 'Unchained Melody' in the car for inspiration. The album included all of their other hits, and at some point, the Righteous Brothers' version of 'White Cliffs Of Dover' came on. I stopped the car in the middle of the street. It had hit me. The record would be released, more or less, on the 50th anniversary of V-E Day. Both Robson and Jerome played soldiers on television. We could put 'White Cliffs Of Dover' on the flip side and make it a double A side. God was smiling on me that day.

RCA was nervous. It had been months since Robson and Jerome had sung 'Unchained Melody' on the show, and the executives weren't certain the public would still care. I forged ahead. I was absolutely insane with conviction. In those days, a big-selling No. 1 single sold about 150,000 copies in the first week. We were shipping about 100,000 copies, so we were well on course to have a Top 5 single. On the morning of the release, I logged in at work to check on repeat orders – in other words, to see how many additional people wanted the record beyond that initial shipment. The figure was astonishing. It was 1.2 million – by lunchtime! The song was going to be No. 1 by a mile – my first No. 1. And while I worried about the week after that, and the week after that, I didn't need to – it stayed at No. 1 for seven weeks. Robson and Jerome were so thrilled that they even agreed to go on *Top of the Pops*, after all. I knew they would.

The second single we released was another double A side, with 'I Believe' and 'Up On The Roof'. When it came out, I sat down with my head of promotions and asked what the biggest rated show on television was. *The National Lottery Show*, he said. So I phoned up the producer of The National Lottery and offered him an exclusive opportunity to have Robson and Jerome sing their new single on the show. He agreed. Sixteen million people were watching, and as a result the second single sold 1.1 million in its first week and stayed at the top of the charts for a month. Everything had happened so quickly that I still had no contract signed with them, even though we'd had two No. 1 singles. I began to get nervous that another label would steal them. When I called them up to talk about it, Robson said, 'I've been waiting for this call. We're in a hotel. Come and meet us.' I was petrified. As it turned out, all they wanted was a fair royalty on the video, which I was more than prepared to give. We all shook hands, and it was then I realized that these guys were two of the most honourable people I had ever met in my life. Almost any other artist would have tried to screw me for another million pounds and I would have had to pay them. But Robson and Jerome were absolutely true to their word.

We put the album out, and it was the best-selling record of 1995. We had the best-selling album again the following year, and at the end of the second album I sat down with them and offered to write them a three million-pound cheque for a third record. Robson smiled. 'Simon,' he said, 'you've made us a lot of money and we've enjoyed it, but we're actors, and this time we're going to say goodbye.'

I was disappointed, but it had been an incredible experience. Robson and Jerome were a class act. For starters, they were in their thirties, and they had all the poise and presence and integrity I could have hoped for. They also made me my first million, which was fantastic, not necessarily because of the money – I didn't think it was enough – but because for the very first time people began to take me seriously. Robson and Jerome really proved to me the power of television and music: seven million albums, five million singles, three million videos. No radio play! We had managed this massive success solely with television and clever marketing, and in the end the whole process taught me what was possible for labels if they sold directly to the public. I still look back on that period as one of the best times of my life. It was innocent and exciting and a very personal success. We went against the prevailing wisdom, made us all millions, and made an absolute fortune for BMG. It was at this point in my career that Radio 1 labelled me the Antichrist of the music industry.

Despite such phenomenal success, I have to admit to making a few mistakes along the way. My biggest regret was not signing the Spice Girls. Simon Fuller, whom I went on to work with on *Pop Idol*, became their manager. I was tipped off, even before Simon, that there was a girl band called Spice, as they were then called, looking for a record deal.

I brought up Spice at an A&R meeting at BMG and there were a lot of furtive looks. It transpired that two of the guys at the company were already chasing the deal. So I backed off. Months later, I bumped into the girls in London and they dragged me into their van and played me their first single. At this point, BMG had apparently backed off the group. I thought the record was sensational. I flew back to the office and got on the phone to Simon, who had recently begun representing them. 'If you haven't cut the deal,' I told him, 'I will literally double whatever anyone has offered.'

'I signed the deal yesterday,' he replied.

Three months later, the Spice Girls exploded onto the scene with their first song, 'Wannabe'.

In retaliation I hired the guy who had put the Spice Girls together, Chris Herbert. I told him that if he had done it once, he could do it again. I initially gave him £25,000 and he put together the band Five – essentially the male equivalent of the Spice Girls. Five went on to sell 1.5 million albums in America and more than ten million records around the world. It made me feel a little better. I have to say that Five were one of my favourite bands I have worked with. I thought they were sometimes brats, but they also were incredibly funny. They would literally beat each other up on the road, but on stage they were sensational. We could have made Five the biggest band on the planet if two things had gone my way.

The first was when the president of Arista Records in the US played me a song submitted to and neglected by TLC. The song was called 'Baby One More Time'. I don't think I've ever heard such a brilliant pop song in my life. He knew I would love the song and I immediately called the writer Max Martin.

'Max,' I said, 'you have to give me this song for Five.'

'I can't,' he said, 'I've promised it to a new singer called Britney Spears.'

'No one's going to have a hit with a stupid name like that!' I screamed. 'Give me the song and I'll ship a brand new Mercedes 600SL to you in 24 hours.'

'Sorry, Simon,' he replied, 'I've given my word.'

Nine months later I met with Max in New York and pleaded with him to work on Five's new album. He agreed and told me he had a great song in mind. I flew back to London, met the band and told them they would fly to Sweden the following weekend to record a new song. The band flew out and within two hours of them entering the studio I got a call from Max. 'The band have walked out. They hate the new song.'

'Play it to me down the phone,' I asked. The song was 'Bye Bye Bye', the song that later broke 'N Sync.

Luckily for my delicate ego, my next signing was the band Westlife – by far the most successful artists I have signed to date.

In June 1999 I got a call from a manager called Louis Walsh. At the time, Louis was famous for putting together BoyZone and had a reputation for being one of the best managers around. We had crossed paths before but had never really worked together. On the phone, he sounded really excited, saying I should come to Ireland immediately because he had put together a fantastic boy band called IOU. The name was enough to put me off right away. He went on, enthusiastically saying they were six Irish lads with the best voices he had ever heard. I asked Louis what they looked like. 'Amazing, just amazing,' was all he said.

The following morning I got on a plane and flew to Dublin, where I booked a big hotel suite. When Louis walked into the room with the six band members, my first thought was, 'He's got to be kidding me.' I thought some of them were really ugly.

But when they started singing, I realized that two of them at least had great voices. Mark was sensational, and I thought Kian looked like the perfect pop star. But I felt, in visual terms, the group would never work.

As they left my suite, I told Louis I thought he was out of his mind. 'I'm not signing the band,' I told him flatly, 'I just can't market them, they look all wrong. Why don't you just keep Kian and Mark and get some other better-looking members?'

'No,' replied Louis, 'I'm afraid I'm not going to do that, I'm going to stick with them.'

I told him if he changed his mind to call me. But by that time he had had enough of me.

Two months later I got an even more animated phone call from Louis, saying, 'I've done it; I've changed the line-up – come and see. I've got rid of four of them and I've brought in some new members.'

I flew back to Dublin the following day to see yet another showcase. Usually, a showcase is paid for by a manager to give you the opportunity to meet the artist. Normally, you're unsure, or you need time to think about it afterwards.

Not this time, though. The new line-up walked on stage and less than 30 seconds into the opening song, I turned to Louis and said, 'This is just amazing.' They looked fantastic, they sounded fantastic. I just knew instinctively what I could do with these boys.

After they finished the showcase, we went upstairs for a cup of tea. I soon discovered that they were also incredibly knowledgeable about the business and knew how they wanted to be marketed. I agreed to commit to the project there and then. I offered them a five-year deal, a five-album deal and told them we would start in the studio within a month. Everyone was really excited.

That day I flew back from Dublin and went straight to Louis's lawyer's office. I didn't want to waste any time. We cut the deal that afternoon.

A little later, I was looking at some photographs of the band and one of the guys with blonde hair seemed really familiar. I turned to Louis and asked him why he looked so familiar. Louis said nothing. I thought I was going nuts.

'Yes, he is familiar,' Louis eventually replied, smirking. 'He was one of the original members. The thing was, I always believed in him, he looked terrible on the day you saw him so I got him to dye his hair blond.'

It was Shane. Poor old Shane, who knew I hated him right from the start, went and dyed his hair blond and was petrified that I was going to spot him – which, of course, I didn't. It was the best thing Louis ever did because he was 100 per cent right. Only Louis Walsh could do that.

One of the first things I did was to change the band's name to Westlife. I got them recording immediately. At that time there was a rumour going around the industry that there was a song available called 'Flying Without Wings', which was written by Steve Mac and Wayne Hector. As I knew Steve fairly well, I called him and asked if he and Wayne could come into my office the next day, because I really wanted to hear the song everyone was talking about. Wayne told me that he had almost promised it to someone in America, but that they would still come in and play it to me.

As soon as I heard it, I knew instinctively that this would be the signature song for Westlife. At that point Westlife were unheard of, so it was hard work convincing Steve and Wayne to choose me over the Americans. I got up, locked my office door, put the key in my pocket and told them they weren't leaving until they gave me the song.

I think it took me two hours to persuade them. And once I got that song, I knew we were almost home and dry. All I needed to do was to get Cheiron, the Swedish production and writing team who had worked with The Backstreet Boys and Britney Spears, to commit to a number of songs. Once I'd done that, I just knew we were going to rule the world with this band – I just knew it. We set up the first single, and the buzz began. Westlife were on their way. We cut the album in six months and I knew it was good. We spent months setting up the first single. For some reason this felt different for me.

On 18 April we flew to Boston for a very important BMG management meeting. We were going to present Westlife to all of the managing directors from around the world. It was a huge deal for us because within all the BMG companies there were massive expectations of Westlife.

I arrived at the weekend, and the following Monday we were due to release the first single, 'Swear It Again'. On Tuesday we were going to get the midweek chart position and that night they were going to perform live. I was excited. If the record went to No. 1 while we were presenting the band to people who could make or break their future success, it would be great news for us.

First thing on Tuesday morning, I phoned up to get the chart position. It was No. 1. I couldn't believe it. I don't think I've ever been so thrilled about a No. 1 record in my life, ever. I just knew instinctively that Westlife would be huge – for them and for me.

The next thing I wanted to do was phone my parents to give them the good news. Mum answered the phone. 'I thought you'd want to know we're No. 1 with Westlife,' I said. She sounded very odd, as though she was out of breath. She didn't say too much and seemed anxious to finish the conversation; it was if she didn't want to speak. I just thought, 'She's obviously in the middle of something.'

I had ordered breakfast when the phone rang. This time it was Nicholas, my younger brother. His voice sounded strained. 'I've got something I have to tell you,' he said 'It's Dad, he died today.'

I couldn't believe it. This was the best day of my life and suddenly it became the worst day of my life. Dad had died from a heart attack, just like that. I had to get home.

Harry Magee, the managing director of RCA came in when he heard the news. I was in pieces, but everyone there treated me so well. The first thing they did was charter me a private jet to go from Boston to New York. From there I would catch Concorde back to Heathrow, which in the end couldn't take off because there was a problem with one of the engines. In a way, I was glad it couldn't take off because it gave me time on my own, just to get myself together.

Eventually, I got a regular flight back to London and drove down to my mother's house in Brighton. It was such a difficult day. It was just a horrible irony what happened on that day, but at the same time it put everything into perspective. All the things I thought were important – chart positions, doing a showcase with the band, and everything else – none of it meant anything any more.

Westlife were in a horrible position, of course, but they were very kind. The boys called me all the time, and in the end I just said to them, 'This is about me and I don't want it to affect you; you've worked very hard for this and you deserve to enjoy your success. Just give me time and everything will be fine.'

It was the worst day I can remember. Looking back on it now, that year was just the start of an incredible journey for me, and it would have been good if Dad could have been there to enjoy at least some of it. After the funneral I took a week off, then went back to work.

Westlife's second single also went in at No. 1. And then I realized we could be heading for something special. At the time, I held the all-time record for consecutive No. 1 singles, something I had achieved with Robson and Jerome. All three of their debut singles went to No. 1. This was then beaten by bloody B*Witched when their first four singles went to No. 1. Westlife's third single also went straight to No. 1. The record was in sight.

Around that time, I went to see the ABBA musical *Mamma Mia* in the West End. Normally, I loathe musicals, absolutely bloody hate them. But everyone had said I ought to go and see this musical so I went along with a girlfriend of mine. For the first half I was totally mesmerized. I thought that it wasn't the best-looking musical on earth, it wasn't a huge production, but the songs made it. Every song was sensational.

During the break I told the girl I was with how inspired I felt by the music. The songs were 20 years old, the theatre was packed and three-year-olds to 80-year-olds knew all the songs. I thought, 'This is what the music business is all about; great songs.' I just knew that something big was about to happen, I didn't know what, but I felt like something was going to happen from watching the ABBA musical. I sat through the second half and just as it was nearing the end, I began to doubt the strange feeling I had had. I thought it was obviously my imagination. Then the last song started, 'I Have A Dream'.

I turned to my girlfriend and said, 'That's it, that's the Christmas No. 1. That's the song I've been waiting for.' She thought I'd gone mad.

Immediately after the show I phoned Louis Walsh and told him what had just happened. I told him we were going to record 'I Have A Dream'. Next, I phoned Pete Waterman, and asked him if he wanted to produce the Christmas No. 1, which would also be the millennium No. 1.

'Absolutely, kiddo,' he said.

Shortly afterwards, Westlife recorded the song and I just knew it was going to be an absolute smash. As luck would have it, ITV were doing an ABBA tribute called *Abba Mania* that year. I arranged for Westlife to be on the show with 'I Have A Dream', and we put the record out for Christmas.

But, unbeknown to us, horror of all horrors, Cliff Richard had made what I consider to be the worst record of all time, 'The Millennium Prayer'. I thought it was ghastly and a bit manipulative. I loathed it. As soon as I heard that record I thought he was going to beat Westlife to the Christmas No.1 I desperately wanted, a) because I wanted four consecutive No. 1 singles, and b) I wanted to have the first No. 1 of the new millennium. It meant everything to me.

Luckily Cliff Richard put his record out early. But he was doing so much publicity. He'd even got himself on *The Royal Variety Show* at the last minute, although Barry Manilow had already been booked to headline the event that year. Because Cliff was No. 1, he got to end the show that night. He also used the fact that the media hated his record. He became the people's champion; everyone felt sorry for Cliff. His press campaign was huge.

I was in Mauritius at the time, pulling my hair out. But when I got the midweek sales figures through on the Tuesday, our sales were astonishingly high. I thought we were definitely going to be the Christmas No. 1.

Soon afterwards, Westlife overtook Cliff Richard to secure the Christmas and millennium No. 1. I can honestly say it's probably the only time in my career when the record industry has cheered one of my No. 1s, because I knocked off the worst record of all time and stopped it from being the millennium No. 1. Westlife's fifth single was released shortly afterwards and went straight to No. 1. We did it. We broke the record.

Westlife went on to have seven consecutive No. 1 singles. One of them was with Mariah Carey – a duet of 'Against All Odds'. Making that record was hilarious. I got a phone call to ask if they would be interested and I said yes. They told me that the song was 'Against All Odds'. I thought it was a brilliant idea, and the boys flew out to Capri to do the vocals. Of course, they came back totally besotted with Mariah.

I was a bit nervous at the time because I thought Westlife would be so in awe of Mariah that it would affect the record. I suspected that she might get them to sing like a lot of Americans who tend to over sing and not keep to the melody. I thought it was very important on this song that we should keep to the original arrangement.

Sure enough, the finished mix came back and I thought it was bloody awful. I phoned up the head of Sony at the time. He asked me what I thought. I said that I loved the idea of it, but that I hated the version. I wanted the boys to go back and redo their vocals and I would have one of our guys mix it.

The head of Sony told me that Mariah would never allow that to happen. I said I wouldn't put the record out unless it was changed. I wasn't taking any chances with a potential sixth consecutive No. 1 single. Eventually Sony came back and asked what I wanted to change. I explained that I wanted Mariah to send me the multi-track and I would redo the vocals in England and mix the record here too. I would then send it to Mariah for approval. Amazingly, she agreed.

I re-recorded the vocals with Steve Mac, and we mixed it together and sent it over to America. At the time Mariah was in Toronto filming *Glitter*. Even though she quite liked the new version, she insisted that the producer and I fly out to talk about some changes. Twenty-four hours later we were on a plane on our way to the studio. Miss Carey kept us waiting an hour-and-a-half. Eventually, she walked in, practically nude, looking amazing and I loved her on sight. I thought, 'You are the epitome of a diva, and you're just going to argue with me for the sake of arguing.' I could see it coming, but there was nothing she could say that was wrong about this record.

Once she had gone through all the changes she wanted, and I wouldn't let her have, there was a terrible silence in the studio. Eventually, she agreed to forget about half the changes she wanted to make. I felt it was partly just about getting her own way. We had a deal, shook hands and then hung out with her for the rest of the evening.

Since then, Westlife have sold about 27 million albums across the world. Working with Westlife is textbook A&R. Absolutely textbook. What I love about the band is that I can always tell them the truth to their faces. The trick to our relationship is that their manager has never stepped in between me and them; he's always allowed us to talk directly. When they have a problem they come to me, and we always speak our minds. That's the reason why they have been so successful. I'd say, half of the meetings we have end up as the most terrible shouting, screaming matches. But no one has ever sulked afterwards or had any bad feelings. There have been times where they could have had me by the throat because they were so annoyed with me. But I have never ever, ever, backed down; I have never said, 'OK, it's five against one.' I have believed in my convictions and stuck to them totally, which has left them incredibly frustrated and angry sometimes, but the minute you start to compromise on a band or an artist, you're finished. Many times we put records out that they felt they wouldn't be No. 1. They hadn't wanted them to come out, but I've convinced them and they have been No. 1; so they know that, in the main, my instincts are good. I should also mention that Westlife happen to be five of the nicest people I have had the pleasure to work with.

I think the lesson with Westlife is, whether you do my job or their job, you have to be like a film director. When a film director works with a very, very talented actor, everybody has to know their place. The difference with most artists who get successful after their first album is that they suddenly want to change direction and they totally miss out; they misunderstand what made them successful in the first place. Whether you're Elvis Presley or Frank Sinatra you're remembered for your songs, and it's the same with Westlife.

As an artist, if you suddenly start believing that as your fans are growing up you've got to chase them, you'll normally find yourself in trouble, you really, really will. That's why I say working with Westlife is textbook A&R, and that's why we've achieved what we have achieved. In my opinion, if Five had had the same attitude as Westlife I could have done exactly the same with them, that's the frustrating thing.

As my most successful artist to date, Westlife are now on their fifth album, which for a pop group is pretty amazing. Westlife's success is due to the fact that they have amazing voices, great charisma, and they put their trust in me and their manager. They haven't tried to change their fan base, they are a vehicle for the songs and it's the songs that have made them successful. That's what they're going to be remembered for in 15 years time, not what they wore or which magazines they appeared in.

I Don't Mean to Be Rude, But...
Sex Sells Only in the Records

I have had two instances where people tried to sell me artists with sex. More than ten years ago, a guy brought a girl into my office. Her name was Maxine. He was her manager, and he looked – and acted – like a second-hand car dealer. She didn't say a word, but just stood there in a long coat while he told me that she was going to be the next Madonna. When he put on her demo it was a joke, and I told them both to forget it.

He said, 'I think we all know what it takes to be a star, and she's good at that. Show him, Maxine.' She then took off her coat to show that she was naked. I had to throw them both out of the office.

Another time, in the wake of the Spice Girls, a manager brought in a new girl band who ran into the office in their underwear, jumped into my lap and made it perfectly clear that they would sleep with me if I signed them.

Neither of those artists got signed. In the higher echelons of the music industry, I think it happens much less than people think. Maybe some guy out at a club says he knows the cousin of an agent, and a girl goes home with him because of it. But not in the real record business. Years ago, when record contracts were £50,000, maybe it was more common, but now a new artist costs two to three million pounds to launch properly. That's an expensive shag.

5

In August 2000 I got a phone call from a television producer at LWT. His name was Nigel Lythgoe, and, as he explained on the telephone, his network had just purchased the rights to an Australian TV programme called *Popstars*. He wanted to meet with me and discuss the possibility of launching the show in England.

We met for lunch at The Ivy in Covent Garden, where Nigel told me about the show. It was divided into two parts, he explained, the first of which was a huge talent show where thousands of singers auditioned, five of whom were eventually selected to form a pop band. The second part of the show was a documentary that followed the band's first days: the tours, the squabbles, and, most importantly, the making of the debut record, which would be released to coincide with the final episode. Nigel asked if I would like to head the panel of judges, and I agreed on one condition – that I would have the recording rights to the band. We didn't have a timetable or a contract, only a productive lunch, and I left the meeting intrigued and excited by the idea.

A few days later, though, I started to have misgivings. For starters, I was worried that the show would expose too much of the music business, that the public didn't need to know the backstage secrets of assembling and promoting a band. I felt it would be the same as going to a magic show and seeing the magician take off his hat, lay down his wand and pedantically explain how he saws his assistant in half. Then there was the question of whether the public even wanted to know. This wasn't a documentary on the manufacturing of pop stardom, after all, but an entertainment show. And, to be perfectly frank, I wasn't thrilled by the prospect of appearing on TV, either.

When I called Nigel back a few weeks later, it was to express my regret that I wouldn't be participating in the show. I spoke to him and to the head of business affairs at Granada, a guy named Simon Jones, and explained that I was in the middle of a Westlife album, and that my obligations to that album were important. They were very disappointed.

After the Westlife album and a holiday in Barbados, I came back to London. For the first time in a long time, I had returned from a holiday without enthusiasm. Normally, after a December trip, my only holiday each year, I come back refreshed and rejuvenated. Because my house was being refurbished I was living at the Mandarin Oriental hotel and that winter I was bored. The whole process, and, for that matter, the whole industry, was becoming too predictable. When I had started making pop records 15 years earlier, only a few labels were releasing the same kind of music. But my success and the success of others had touched off a kind of pop epidemic. Suddenly, pop music was in vogue, and profiteers of all shapes and sizes were flocking to it for an easy buck. It was at that time that I saw a billboard for *Popstars*. My heart sank.

I watched the first two episodes and I knew I had made a huge mistake. The show was fantastic. It had everything I thought was missing from the pop world at that time: excitement, spontaneity and risk. The people on the judging panel were good. Nigel was funny, Nicki diplomatic and the A&R guy quiet. However, I knew after the first viewing that they were on to a winning formula. I knew that the label was going to sell an awful lot of records by whatever band came out of the show. I remember turning around to Louise, my girlfriend at the time, and saying, 'Fuck, I have made a huge mistake.'

I first met Louise at an awards function. I was eating and my fork was suspended in mid-air as this girl walked in. I remember saying to whoever I was sitting with, 'You have got to find out who this girl is – now.' She was a model, so Kim, who was married to my brother Nicholas at the time and was also a model, was sent on a mission to try and get me a date with this girl. I was mental over her for almost a year, which is how long it took to fix us up. We arranged to have dinner. The night I took her out I came down with the worst flu I've ever had in my life. I was shivering so much I could hardly keep my fork still. She ended up inviting me back to her place and I just couldn't stay. I felt pathetic. Two days later she came over for lunch and I was completely tongue-tied. I think I liked her too much. Every time I tried to make things better, it just got worse; that afternoon she just kind of huffed off and didn't return my calls.

A year later, I learned that she had split up with a guy she had met after my pitiful attempt to date her. I called her and she agreed to have dinner with me. This time, everything went well and I managed to speak coherently throughout dinner. We dated for about five months and got engaged in New York. It happened very, very quickly. When we came back and I told everyone I was engaged, no one could believe I was going to get married. Fairly soon afterwards, we realized it wasn't going to work; I was incredibly busy with my label and would work for 14–16 hours most days. We were both very pragmatic about it. While we were really into each other, it wasn't right. Louise wanted a stable home life and kids, and I knew that an important phase of my career was just starting, so we agreed we weren't going to get married. It was very difficult.

Just after that, I went on holiday and missed her like crazy, so I came back and pursued her like a madman all over again. The second time round, we lasted nearly a year, and after that we dated a third time. It was very rocky, very rewarding and very important. She is now married with a baby. Louise has a great sense of humour, one of the best I've ever known. She has always been able to make me laugh. But we both knew it would never have worked. She will always be a good friend.

I kept watching that first season of *Popstars*, in part because Louise was hooked and I found myself obsessively analysing the show – on its failures as well as its successes. One of the failures, I felt, was that once the audition process ended, the nature of the show changed significantly, and not for the better. I remember thinking at the time, too, that the show suffered a bit by having a group at its core. It would have been more compelling if it focused on a solo star. The major flaw was easy to spot. The hook of the show was the suspense in not knowing who was going to be picked. But as the band were chosen two-thirds of the way through the show's run, you lost that element. It was obvious that it would have been more exciting to announce the winner at the end of a show like this.

Just before I went to Barbados, Simon Fuller came up to me at the Record of the Year celebrations – Westlife had won for the second year running – and told me that he wanted to work with me the following year. Interestingly my boss at BMG, Richard Griffiths, had said I should hook up with Simon because he believed we would work well together. Simon was riding high from his success with the Spice Girls, but he was never one to rest on his laurels, and he was already starting to think ahead to the next challenge. Over the years, Simon and I had occasionally spoken about working together. In fact, two or three years before, while we were both on holiday in Mauritius, we had talked at length about collaborating. During that conversation, we found that our tastes were eerily similar. In fact, at one point, we were talking about our favourite authors, and we both mentioned Tom Sharpe – what was more, we had both started reading the new Tom Sharpe book at exactly the same time and had given up on the same chapter at the same time. 'You know,' I remember telling him, 'if we ever did a project together, it would be bigger than the Spice Girls.' Bearing in mind the Spice Girls had sold over 35 million records, that was quite a declaration, but I had a feeling. I was certain that something would happen in the not too distant future that would put the two of us together. The Record of the Year meeting was the catalyst. While we had, between the two of us, more or less owned UK pop music for the previous five or six years, the success of *Popstars* had changed the landscape significantly, and I felt that it was the proper time for us to collaborate. The reservations I had sprung mostly from the fact that we were so similar – we would agree on almost everything, I thought, but if we disagreed, it would be a clash between two control freaks.

At any rate, we decided to have a dinner meeting in January the following year to discuss working together. Suffice to say that Simon went on to create the format for *Pop Idol* and we subsequently entered into an agreement, under which his company would manage the artist and own the television rights and my company would acquire the recording rights. We both believed in the show, we both knew it was going to happen, and worked like crazy over the next six weeks to develop the concept.

During that time it was decided that we would approach a production company to help make the programme, and we settled on FremantleMedia, which was called Pearson at that time. The reason was yet another Simon: Simon Jones, whom I had disappointed when I decided not to judge the first British edition of *Popstars*. He had since left Granada to join Pearson, and he had kept in touch with me. We met

Simon and executive, Alan Boyd, who was instrumental in helping get the show started. I love Alan. Even though he's a very powerful executive, he likes to remember his TV roots. 'I'll put on my leather jacket and meet you in the control room,' he likes to say. He always talks about his leather jacket. When we met Alan, he wrote out all the major details of *Pop Idol* on an envelope that he still carries around with him today.

From the start, we knew that the *Pop Idol* concept depended on the relationships between the four judges. I was going to be one of the judges, which I had mixed feelings about. From the start, I envisaged that Pete Waterman would be one of the other judges. As I had known Pete for years, I knew that we worked well together, even when we disagreed, and that would make for good television.

This was true in theory, but it was also true in fact. Years before, a man named Paul Smith, who ran a TV company called Celador, had come to see me about a new television programme. 'Simon,' he said, 'we're developing a show called *Who Wants To Be A Millionaire*? It's costing us quite a lot of money, and we're a bit nervous. We want to do something to publicize the show in advance.'

'Where do I fit in?' I asked.

'Can you help us make the theme music?' he said.

I was sceptical. I didn't see that anyone would want to buy the theme music to a game show. But I thought that if anyone could make a theme song that would also be a pop hit, it would be Pete Waterman. I phoned him up and asked him to come in for a meeting with the Celador executives.

So there we were: Pete and I, along with a number of top executives from Celador. The meeting went smoothly for about four minutes, at which point Pete and I started having a huge row over what the song should be. The TV executives just sat there in stunned silence. I'm sure they had never heard anything like it in their lives, two grown men screaming at each other at the top of their lungs. Eventually, mercifully, the meeting came to an end. 'Simon,' Paul said, 'if you and Pete ever decide to do a TV show together, call me.' That comment stuck in my mind. It lasted longer than either my or Pete's involvement with *Who Wants To Be A Millionaire?*; we never did create the theme music for the show.

Once the press started to report that Simon and I were developing an idea, other celebrities and record-industry personalities began to show interest in judging on the show. I wasn't interested in many of them, but then I got a phone call from Neil Fox. 'If it's true you're doing the show I'd love to be on the panel,' he said. Neil had started off as a DJ in a tiny little station in Wyvern, and then moved on to Radio Luxembourg and eventually to Capital Radio, where he did a daily programme called *The Big Drive Home* and a Sunday Top 40 countdown. I had always liked Neil. He was very enthusiastic and I remember thinking that he would be perfect.

That only left the issue of the fourth judge. Everyone was in agreement that we needed a girl to complete the panel. Since the beginning, in fact, Simon Fuller had proceeded with a very specific girl in mind – Nicki Chapman. Nicki had started her career as a music-industry publicist, and had worked with me for years at BMG. She started her own promotions company called Brilliant Promotions and after a few years joined 19. There was some concern over repeating personnel from the earlier show, but it was dispelled quickly enough, and, just like that, we had our four judges.

Armed with the concept and the cast, the show was ready to be sold. Between us, Simon and I had sold hundreds of millions of records, and Simon had even had success with his S Club TV show. Still, I was nervous. We were set to meet Claudia Rosencrantz at ITV, one of the toughest executives in the business, and even though she had commissioned the original *Popstars*, television sales are never easy. We all trooped in for a meeting and Simon and I went through the beginning of our extremely well-rehearsed pitch. About two minutes into it, Claudia put up her hand and said, 'Stop.'

My heart sank.

'I'll take it,' she said.

'What?' Simon and I said at the same time.

'I'll take it,' she said. 'I love it, I think it's absolutely brilliant. Who's the panel?'

We told her, slowly, perhaps, given our stunned state.

'Perfect,' she said. 'I'll have it on air in the autumn.'

We couldn't believe it. The show had been sold on the first try. As it turned out, we had also scheduled a meeting with the BBC, and, out of respect to them, we decided to go ahead and keep the appointment. We decided that Alan Boyd, from FremantleMedia, and I would make the same pitch to the BBC. And they listened carefully. They didn't jump up and down, but they were interested. 'Look,' I finally said, 'I have to be honest with you. I am pretty sure there is a deal over at ITV. I think they're very interested in this show.'

'We understand,' they said. 'We'll get back to you tomorrow.' I'm sure they thought I was bullshitting them.

The next day, the phone went absolutely crazy. Most of the calls were from the BBC; they had thought more about the idea and wanted it. We were suddenly in an enviable but difficult position, with two offers from two different networks. It was resolved in the only decent way – a deal was done with the first offer. The BBC was interested and generous, but ITV had spoken up first. Plus, they had the experience of *Popstars*.

* * *

The first month of production wasn't exactly smooth. The television people took umbrage that the record-industry people were encroaching upon their space, and the record-industry people couldn't stop reminding the television people that an understanding of the music business was a prerequisite for *Pop Idol*. In my case, I tangled early and often with Richard Holloway, one of the executive producers. We were a bit like two dogs in the park, and it took us a while actually to realize we liked and respected each other. These days, I count him as one of my closest friends in the television business, but in the early days it was very confrontational.

Soon enough, we had ironed out everything. We had figured out the details of the staging. We had worked out the specifics of the recording contract we would offer the winner. We had hired our executive producers: Richard Holloway, Kenny Warwick, and, last but not least, Nigel Lythgoe, who now joined 19 to head up their television division. When we released an announcement to the press, Simon and I were sure that everyone would jump right on the story. We were sure it would be front-page news. Instead, no one cared. A few small stories were written, but nothing substantial.

6

We approached the *News of the World* to advertise the audition dates and they were very enthusiastic about being involved. Once the show was outlined they got it very quickly. This helped us attract a decent amount of people to apply. After all the months of preparation, the time had come for the auditions. We flew up to Manchester, hired cars from the airport, set ourselves up in the audition room and waited for the first singer. I'd like to report that it was a historic moment, but the truth is that we were all a bit ill at ease and totally useless as a panel. We had no chemistry; maybe we were too aware of the cameras. The problem was it felt false.

Initially we judged the contestants after they had sung and left the room. We deliberated, called the contestant back and told them what we thought. It didn't work.

'It's not working.' Nigel said.

'It's not real,' I told him.

'Then do what you would normally do. Tell the contestant what you think straight after they have sung,' he said.

We tried that approach, and it was better, but there was still something missing. Our politeness was so thick that it was almost palpable. I called for a break and asked Pete to take a walk with me outside. 'You know,' I said. 'I'm dying in there. I'm not saying what I would say to them in a normal audition. I think we have to be ourselves.'

'I agree,' Pete said. It was then that I realized that in the manic months of preparation, we had entirely forgotten to discuss what we were going to do in the audition room.

The next person who came in sang terribly. And we told him! There was silence in the room. The singer walked out and was followed by someone else who was even worse. Again we told them the truth.

After a sticky star the first day was great. I realized we had something special. There was comedy (unintentional), talent, drama and tantrums, tears and joy. In other words, it was like a real-life audition. I thought the chemistry of the panel now worked. I was convinced the TV audience would love the show. It felt like a musical Lions and the Christians.

* * *

Of course, apart from us there were the contestants. The first day in Manchester we met Zoe Birkett. She was only 16 years old and I thought she was sensational. She was raw and a little unpolished as a performer, but she was cute and she had a great voice. She reminded me a bit of a young Whitney Houston. After meeting Zoe I looked over at Nigel who was smiling. The whole show suddenly came together: we could be outspoken when the contestants' talent – or lack of – warranted it, and then we could be genuinely excited and enthusiastic when someone like Zoe lit up the room.

That day was also the first time I met Gareth Gates. Sometimes there are performers that hook you from the first time you see them. As soon as Gareth walked in the room, I remember praying that he would have a fantastic voice. There was just something so compelling about him; I knew that girls would go mental over him. 'What's your name?' I asked.

He was silent. I stared at him. Then I realized he wasn't silent at all. He was trying to talk, but he had a stutter – a fairly severe one – and he couldn't get the words out. The footage that aired on television was heavily edited; there in the room, Gareth took nearly ten minutes.

I couldn't believe it. I wanted this great-looking kid to sing in front of four bored-looking judges, but it had taken him ten minutes to say his name. I remember thinking how brave he was to sing for us. I asked him what he was going to sing and again it took him ages to say 'Flying Without Wings'.

I don't think it's an exaggeration to say that every hair on the back of my neck and on my arms just stood up straight. I knew the song and knew it well – Westlife had recorded it and taken it to No. 1 – and it was clear to me from the first note that Gareth was very good. Everything we had just witnessed prior to him singing made his performance quite emotional for all of us. I remember holding my hand up to say stop. He stood there, petrified. 'You are 100 per cent coming to London for the next round,' I said. His smile lit up the room and the other judges echoed my praise. From that moment, he was the No. 1 frontrunner; I thought to myself that we had not only a successful show, but also a potential star. I remember phoning Simon in France that evening and telling him about Gareth. 'You've got a hit show and a hit artist,' I said.

After Manchester, spirits were high. We were confident about our roles as judges. We were able to be ourselves and that is crucial. Now, I know that in the years since that first season – and especially since the show's success in America – I have been thought of as the mean judge. But to be honest, in those first days I was anything but cruel. Pete was, and always has been, more unpleasant than I am. I'm probably funnier than he is, but he's indisputably crueller. Neil was brought in because he was optimistic to a fault – I used to call him 'H-A-P-P-Y Radio' – and Nicki balanced us out. It had worked.

The second city we visited was Glasgow and soon there was a buzz among the production crew. The cause? Darius Danesh was there. Darius, of course, was the laughing stock of England as a result of his appearance on *Popstars*, where he gave one of the worst auditions ever televised. Nothing defined the phrase 'musical train wreck' better than Darius Danesh singing 'Baby One More Time'. 'What the hell is he doing here?' I asked. Still, I was intrigued by Darius; I figured that he was either the biggest idiot on earth, or one of the bravest people I would ever have the pleasure of meeting. Either way, he had the power to create excitement, and that was something. When he walked in to the audition, he asked the judges if he could perform with a guitar.

'No,' I said, 'you can't use a guitar. No one's using instruments.'

'Well, I've prepared a song on the guitar,' he said.

'Well, then, you're not auditioning,' I said.

'OK, OK,' he said. 'I'll just sing a song.' He sang a Seal song, and it wasn't bad at all. He was a good-looking boy with a good voice, and he had some charisma. The other judges agreed, and we put him through. He was absolutely thrilled, and so was I. I really thought Darius would add something to the show. Unfortunately, not everyone we met along the way could sing as well as Gareth, Zoe or Darius. I was amazed to find most of them were absolutely useless and yet everyone believed they were great. I couldn't believe it. We were listening to some of the worst singers I have ever heard. But one of these awful singers turned out to be a part of *Pop Idol* history. Caroline Buckley was so dippy she turned up for the audition thinking it was for an MTV presenter. When she was told it was a singing audition she sang the first song that came into her head: 'YMCA'. The rest is history.

I Don't Mean to Be Rude, But...
Disco Was the Only Time for Great Dance Music

I always think that whenever you compare the music of the era you grew up in to the music of today, you sound like a boring old fart. But I genuinely believe that the disco era was one of the best times for pop music – ever. It was an era that encouraged fun, glamour and excess. It was camp but sexy, and some of the best dance records of all time came out of that movement, from Chic's 'Good Times' and 'Le Freak' to Donna Summer's classic 'I Feel Love'. The lyrics were mostly about having a good time, and in that pre-AIDS culture, sex appeal was extremely impor- tant. Disco exploded worldwide when the Bee Gees performed and wrote the soundtrack to Saturday Night Fever. *After that*

*– shock-horror – boys started dancing in clubs. For three years,
from 1977 to 1980, disco ruled the world. Even artists like Rod
Stewart got in on the act by making disco singles. Rod had one
of his biggest hits ever with the disco version of 'Do Ya Think I'm
Sexy'. Today, 25 years later, the songs still sound amazing, and
I wonder, if* Pop Idol *is around 30 years from now, will we
devote a week to the Wu Tang Clan?*

On the final day in London, one of the producers came
in and told us that we had a bit of a problem.
Evidently, we had more girls than guys. 'If you're on the
borderline with a singer,' this producer said, 'and it's a guy,
try to put them through.' That very first season had many
of these situations; we were learning as we went along. So
the very last person of the entire audition process walked in
– a boy wearing a funny old jumper with a stain on it and
baggy jeans.

'What's your name?' I said.

'Will,' he said. 'Will Young.'

'What are you going to sing, Will?'

'"Blame It On The Boogie" by the Jackson Five,' he
said. It was a dance song, of course, and Will wasn't a great
dancer, but he had a good enough voice. I looked over to
Nigel Lythgoe, who was standing off to the side, and he
nodded to me. We put him through; to be honest, even a few

days later, I didn't remember him. I did remember thinking he reminded me of Howard from Take That.

The favourites at that point were Gareth Gates, Zoe Birkett and Rosie Ribbons. The only wildcard, really, was a guy named Rik Waller, who we had seen in Manchester. He was a nice enough kid, but when he came in we all did a double-take, because his image wasn't what you would think of as a traditional pop-star image. Rick, you see, was huge. Then he sang, and he just blew us away. He had an absolutely amazing voice, and he went through to the finals in a flash.

At that point, we had to narrow our pool of 120 singers down to 50. It was fairly simple, and we were moving along. Then, during the second day of auditions, Nigel Lythgoe came up to me. 'There's something I have to tell you,' he said. 'Alone.' He was absolutely ashen, and the first thing I thought was that someone in my family had died.

We went off to one side. 'What's the matter?' I said.

'A plane crashed into the World Trade Center in New York,' he said.

'You're kidding me,' I said.

'No,' he said. 'I just heard it on the news. It's stuck in the tower, burning.'

'Well,' I said. 'What do you want us to do? Should we stop?'

With my first girlfriend. This must have been when
I started wearing high-waisted trousers.

Tony, Mum, Dad, Nicholas and Me
on holiday in Bermuda 1964

With Nicholas when he still
believed in Father Christmas

In the garden with Mum and Nicholas

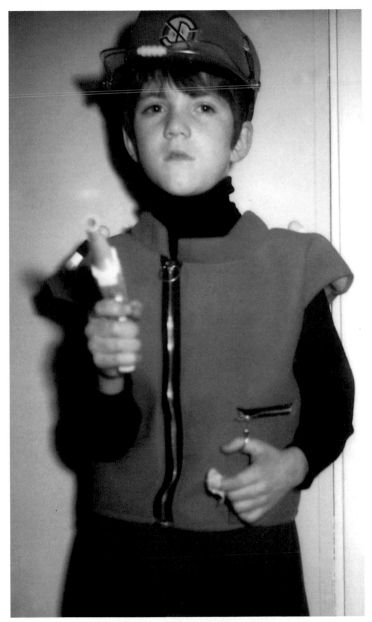

Aged 7 as Capital Scarlet

Worst haircuts ever

Me and Dad. It would have been good if Dad could have been here to enjoy at least some of my success.

'Don't you start being rude...' warns Mum.

'We can't,' Nigel said. 'We've got to carry on filming. It's the only time we've got the theatre.'

A few minutes later, Nigel was back. 'Simon,' he said, 'a second plane has just gone into the Trade Center. They think it might be terrorists.'

Now I was really worried. 'Nigel,' I said, 'I'm not sure I want to do this now.'

'Please try,' he said. 'We've just got to get through it as quickly as possible.' I went back and explained the situation to the other judges, and we moved things along as quickly as possible. The kids probably thought we were mad: we were pushing them to go faster, faster. Then, just after we got out of the building, Nigel's cell phone rang. It was his son, who had just heard a report that six unidentified planes were on their way to London. At that point, of course, there were false rumours everywhere. Some of the kids were also getting calls and hearing rumours, and the fear was suddenly everywhere. Nigel and I went back to my house and watched CNN. I remember saying to Nigel, 'This puts things into perspective. We've been wrapped up in a talent competition and then you see this.' I know this sounds trite, but I think everyone was thinking those kinds of thoughts. It was very, very difficult to go back that night and finish the deliberations – hard on us, hard on the kids and hard on the producers. After a very difficult day we had our top 50. It was obvious that there was also one clear favourite: Gareth. The other front-runners were Rosie Ribbons (who made Pete cry in the auditions), Rik Waller (who made Pete go mental because he didn't think a fat person could be a Pop Idol), Zoe Birkett, who had been very good in the last audition, and, of course, Darius, our dark horse. When we were deliberating from 100 to 70, we created a 'maybe' room. This was for people we couldn't really decide on. One of the occupants was a certain Will Young. Will just hadn't entered our radar. I remember the deliberations when we had to agree on the final 50 and Will's name came up. Nobody had championed him because at this stage he hadn't shone. I really thought at this point the competition would be between Gareth, Zoe, Rosie and Rik Waller.

As soon as we had completed the UK auditions we decided to fly to America to see if we could sell the show to a US network. I flew out with Simon Fuller and Simon Jones. The three Simons. Though we left Britain with the highest hopes for selling the show, we realized soon after arriving in America that this wasn't going to be quite as easy as we'd thought. Our first meeting was with one of the smaller US networks. I can't say which, but it was a network that wasn't doing well at the time, and we figured that they needed a show like *Pop Idol* to jump-start their ratings. It was decided that only Simon Jones and myself would attend the meeting. The meeting was a complete disaster from start to finish. The boss of the network was flanked by two so-called entertainment experts. I had been selected to make the pitch, and I thought I had done a brilliant job. I had talked up the whole concept of *Pop Idol*, explained the network's earning potential from telephone voting, and concluded that the show would revolutionize music and talent, all on American television. When I had finished speaking, there was a terrible silence. It went on for a second, then a minute, then an hour – well, maybe not, but it seemed like an hour. Finally, and without any emotion whatsoever, one of the executives just looked at me blankly. 'So,' he said, 'what exactly do you want us to do for you?'

'Actually,' I said, 'it's more a question of what we could do for you.' Another silence followed. This one was even longer. At this point I realized that they just didn't get it, and that there was no sense in continuing with the meeting. Simon Jones attempted to re-ignite the conversation but it all fell on completely deaf ears. In the end we were more or less asked to leave. Going down in the lift, the other Simon was glum, but I couldn't stop myself from laughing. The response to the pitch just struck me as ludicrous. I was so confident that the concept would be sold to the highest bidder, and that the network we had just met had lost out on the chance of a lifetime. 'This place wouldn't have suited us anyway,' I assured him.

Our second meeting, the following day, was with executives from one of the largest TV networks in the United

States. When Simon Jones and I arrived for the meeting, I was dazzled by the size of the company's headquarters. It was more than large; it was the most intimidating place I have ever seen. They kept us waiting in the reception area for almost an hour. I could see that the other Simon was getting anxious.

Eventually a young, tired-looking executive emerged and led us into a tiny office in the deepest recesses of the building. A monstrously small office in a monstrously big building – the three of us were so cramped at the table that our shoulders touched. I started the pitch. I explained *Pop Idol*. I explained the American Dream. I explained the ins and outs of telephone voting, both as a democratic ideal and as a revenue stream. Or rather, I started to explain. Halfway through that part of my pitch, the executive suddenly held his hand up and said, 'No.'

'Er,' I said. It's rare that I'm speechless. 'I'm sorry, but I haven't finished yet. Don't you want to hear the rest of it?'

'No.'

'Why not?' I demanded.

'Because it's a music show,' he said. He sounded exhausted. I was flabbergasted, and underneath the table I kicked Simon Jones to let him know it. The meeting was awful. The climate was awful. The man was awful. I just wanted to leave. I took one last stab, asking if he really meant no when he said no, if he was telling me, in no uncertain terms, that his company would never buy the show. 'Yes,' he said, 'I am saying that. It's just not for us, I'm afraid.'

After the first meeting, I had laughed, not because I was keeping up a brave front, but because it had never even occurred to me that the show wouldn't sell in the US. After the second meeting, I sat down on the steps of the huge office building and put my head in my hands. I felt as tired as the executive who had said 'No.' Simon Jones was despondent and I had made things worse – not with my pitch, which I thought was good despite the man's negativity, but because I had forgotten to order a car to pick us up. For the first time, the possibility of failure came across me like a chill. What if no one recognized the enormous potential of the show? What if no one understood that American viewers were primed for this kind of experience? That night, we met Simon Fuller who was amazed at the lack of interest. He wasn't as down as us and was convinced one of the networks would eventually commit. I wasn't so sure.

No deal for the show was done by the time we left Los Angeles.

Before the first episode of *Pop Idol* was aired, we had a press conference; it was the first time I was introduced to the media. When I got there everyone was swarming around Nicki, because of her role on *Popstars*. Everyone knew Pete because he has always been a big public figure in the record industry. And everyone knew Neil, because he's a famous DJ. No one was talking to me. As part of the press conference, we were going to show the assembled media a 15-minute tape of the show. This was the first I had seen of the show, as well, and as far as I was concerned it was make or break for us. I remember sitting there just enthralled by the tape; after it finished, there was silence, followed by the biggest round of applause you have ever heard in your life. I turned around to Pete and said, 'This show is going to be massive.'

To reinforce this, Mark Frith, the editor of *Heat*, walked up to me and said, 'Congratulations, you have a hit.'

The show aired a few weeks later. It was great TV. I forgot the fact I was in it; I just loved the show. And if I loved it, I thought, an awful lot of other people would love it too. I was right.

There were so many reasons why the show was great. It was funny, authentic and, of course, we had our secret weapon, Ant and Dec. They are, in my opinion, the best television double act since Morecambe and Wise. They have always been absolutely brilliant, and when ITV told me that they had signed them, I was thrilled. They're not best friends of mine, so I'm not saying this to be sycophantic, but I think that if I had to pinpoint one reason why this show worked so well, especially at the beginning, I would begrudgingly admit that Ant and Dec made the difference. I watched them on that first show, just like everybody else, and I remember thinking how brilliant they were and how lucky I was to have them on the show.

As the first episodes were going out live, we were preparing to film the middle section, in which the finalists we had selected would perform live. Here our first real problems arose. I had always assumed that the four of us would judge the competition until the end. We were an integral part of the formula. There was no tension without us. Despite that, one of the producers said to me, 'Simon, we need to talk to you about the role you play when we go into this round.'

'What do you mean "role"?' I said.

'Well,' he said. 'We'd like you to come down and offer some encouragement once a week.'

'What are you talking about?'

'Well,' he said, 'there's no judging after the audition shows.'

'According to who?' I said.

'It was never assumed that you would judge this until the end,' he said.

'Of course it was,' I said. 'Don't be an idiot.' But as it turned out, I was the idiot, as least for a little while. There was a consensus that the judges should be removed from this phase, and I was actually taken out for lunch by a couple of the producers, who told me that they thought that judging was only appropriate for the audition phase, not the performance phase.

'Well,' I said, 'what will happen when the contestants walk out?'

'Nothing,' a producer said.

'That's right,' I said. 'Nothing. You're making a big mistake here. I don't think we should make a decision on this yet, not because I necessarily want to stay on television, but because without the judges we lose the heart of the show.'

I was amazed that at this point, so deep into the show, this issue wasn't yet resolved.

One of the things I did before the show aired was hire a media consultant. I realized I might need some help controlling the media. Why? Well, for starters, I was 41 years old. I had 25 years of relationships behind me, and I had a feeling that if I suddenly became a public figure, there might be one or two kiss and tells coming out of the woodwork. As far as I was concerned, there was only one person to talk to, and that was Max Clifford. I called his assistant, made an appointment and the next day I went down to his offices on New Bond Street. I was a bit nervous when I walked in – he has a fearsome reputation – but he was friendly from the start. 'Sit down, Simon,' he said. 'Why are you here?'

'I'm going to judge this new show called *Pop Idol*,' I said, 'and I think it's going to be very popular but somewhat controversial.' I then explained the show's format.

'Sounds like a great show,' he said. 'Why are you here to see me?'

'Well,' I said, 'I have a hunch that one or two stories about me may appear in the press.'

'Like what?' he said. 'What have you done?'

I told him. He then went through a list of questions.

'Are you single?' he asked me.

'Yes.'

'Never been married?'

'No.'

'Don't have kids?'

'No.'

'You work in the music industry?'

'Yes.'

'Well,' he said, 'what are you worried about?'

'If I get a call from a journalist in the middle of the night,' I said, 'I want to know how to deal with it. I have advised artists all my life, but I don't know the first thing about being in the spotlight myself.'

He agreed to help me – although when he told me what he charged, I nearly fell out of my seat. In retrospect, though, hiring Max was one of the best decisions I have made. He explains things in a very matter-of-fact way; he told me, for example, that if the press gives you publicity you owe it to them to give something back if they want it. Max also took it upon himself to watch *Pop Idol* regularly. If he thought I had acted like a complete arsehole, he would call me and set me straight. He was never sycophantic and his instincts were always right. He was worth every penny.

The first time I ever did a TV talk show interview, in fact, was with Frank Skinner, and I was shit-scared. I knew I was supposed to be entertaining, and that Frank would try to take the piss out of me. Max, who sensed that I was nervous, cleverly dropped by the show with his daughter Louise and some friends. All of them came to my dressing room and we just chatted until it was time for the show. As a result, I thoroughly enjoyed the experience, and I wasn't as bad as I expected.

Max and I have become good friends. That doesn't mean, of course, that he is always nice to me. There was one particular occasion, after two or three kiss and tell stories about me appeared in the tabloids, when I started to feel sorry for myself. I phoned Max and said, 'I'm getting really fed up.' I was beginning to wish I had never started.

Max just laughed. 'You know what your problem is?' he said. 'You're taking yourself too bloody seriously. Think of all the good things that have happened to you over the past few months.' Then he slammed the phone down on me.

'Christ,' I thought, 'he's ruder than I am.' But he was dead right.

The controversy with the judges wasn't yet resolved, but it was about to be. The set of four audition shows ended with the Criterion Show, on which the contestant pool went from 100 down to 50, and that was the only audition show on which the judges were kept away from the contestants. I had got into the habit of watching the show with my friends and my family, and I remember that during that particular show all these people who had watched so intently all along weren't really paying attention. They were talking amongst themselves, getting up, making tea and so forth. They weren't as involved, because the sense of confrontation had gone.

Later that night I received a call from Claudia Rosencrantz at ITV. 'I've just seen the show and I don't like it,' she said. 'Why weren't you guys more involved?'

'Hasn't anyone told you that the judges are no longer on the show?' I said.

'We'll see about that,' she said quietly. A day later the judges were back.

Dear Mr Cowell,

I am not going to ask how you are because I don't care.

I am writing to you because I have just finished watching the 2nd POPIDOL programme and I am extremely annoyed. You are the rudest and conceited man I have ever had the misfortune to watch on television. What do you know about music? NOTHING.

Half of the people you don't like are very talented and I am sure will becomke big stars. Who will have the last laugh then?

I have to warn you I will be watching every single episode of this series and a detailed report will be sent to my MP and the ITV watchdogs. People like you are bad for British culture. You obviously don't remember Hughie Green. He was never rude to anyone.

Yours disgustingly

Miss F

9

The middle section of the show, which extracted the ten finalists from the group of 50, was filmed at a TV studio in Teddington in November 2001. The field would be divided into five performing groups, and the public would pick two singers from each group.

In our first group of ten, Gareth made it clear why he was the red-hot favourite to win. He was in a league of his own. He picked up a huge amount of the vote and Zoe Birkett came second. It was clear also that the two of them were very close.

The second show was fairly uneventful. Hayley Evetts picked up the most votes. She was good, possibly her best performance. Laura Doherty, who we saw in Scotland, also made it through.

* * *

The third live show contained what, for most people watching *Pop Idol*, was one of the show's defining moments. It wasn't the fact that Chris Niblett, a decent singer who we put through, began to perform under the name Korben. No, it had to do with Will Young, and how he responded to my criticism. At that point, Will just wasn't on the radar. No one had championed him. No one was picking him to win. He was just a nice-looking boy with a nice attitude and a good voice. During one of those middle heats, he came on and sang the Doors' 'Light My Fire'. Now, remember that the performances the viewers see on television take place in a radically different context from the one they did while we were filming. The judges only see a singer. The audience at home sees a profile piece on video, then the singing and then the recap in the Green Room with Ant and Dec. In many ways, that additional content can determine whether a singer gets through. Will's performance was a perfect example of this principle. His video was a very nicely edited piece that showed him quietly writing his diary, hoping I wasn't going to criticize him. He spoke very eloquently. I didn't see that, of course, and I didn't care. For some reason that day I was in a bad mood. As a result, when Will stood in front of me and sang this song, the first thing that went through my mind was that I had heard this a million times; it reminded me of somebody at a family gathering, singing round the piano and receiving a polite round of applause. I told him that, and Nicki Chapman then encouraged him to say something back to me. This was probably the most important piece of advice Nicki had ever given anyone in her life. Will looked at me, took a deep breath and then responded. 'I don't think you can ever call that average.' He carried on and very methodically told me I was wrong. He was calm and eloquent.

And of course the kids who were in the Green Room back-stage with Ant and Dec went mad. They loved that someone was standing up to me. I remember thinking how poised he was, how he had thought through his argument so perfectly. I had no choice but to do what I did, which was to look at him and say, 'You are a gentleman, sir.' Then he went into the room with Ant and Dec and made fun of himself, which was also very clever; he said that if he hadn't defended himself, his father would have taken a shotgun to him. When I watched the show back that Saturday night I went pale. It suddenly dawned on me how strong and charming his personality was; even his song sounded better on the TV than it did in the room. In other words, I had got it spectacularly wrong!

The effect had taken hold: Will sailed through. The public had fallen in love with him. He was the boy who gave Simon Cowell a dose of his own medicine.

After Will and I tangled during the live broadcast, the show's ratings went up and the next week featured two very good vocalists. The two winners, as luck would have it, were both Welsh girls: Jessica Garlick and Rosie Ribbons. Jessica was a huge fan of Pete Waterman: she knew everything about his career, and she was almost breathless when he spoke to her. That night, I noticed that Pete's behaviour was changing. He was becoming extremely emotional about some of the kids, almost paternal. When Rosie Ribbons sang, Pete had tears in his eyes. 'God,' I thought. 'You're really a softie at heart.' It was probably because of his old age.

That left only one more group. From that final group, Aaron Bayley went through; he had everything you would want in a singer – except star quality – and while I liked him immensely, I didn't think he had much of a chance. We had only one more finalist to name, and, as luck would have it, Rik Waller was coming up to sing. During Rik's first appearance, I had got into a big argument with Pete Waterman; Pete was still sulking because he had made it through. I was glad Rik had made it through because I would rather have a big guy with a big voice in the competition than an insipid, good-looking wannabe without a personality. Because of how hard I had fought to put him through, I was surprised to hear from the make-up girls that they felt Rik had been acting the big star with everyone back-stage. I felt personally responsible for Rik being there, and I didn't like to hear that he had apparently gone all big-headed and was telling people he was going to win this competition. When he came on for his heat, I spoke to him, right there, on camera. 'I have to say something, Rik,' I said. 'I really hope this hasn't gone to your head, because I liked you and if it starts going to your head, you and I are going to have a problem.' I'd made my point and then I let him sing. I have to say he sang extremely well. His choice of song was fantas-tic, 'I Can't Make You Love Me', which contains a very rele-vant lyric, 'don't patronize me'. All forgiven, Rik. Darius struggled, though. He just lost it. He didn't make it through.

Within a few days, I realized that Will had made a bigger impact than I had thought. Pete Waterman told me that he believed Will would win, and Simon Fuller, too, phoned me to tell me that he thought Will was the one to watch. I still sensed that it was a one-horse race; that Gareth Gates was going to walk away with the title.

Gareth's story, remember, was like something out of a Hollywood movie. He was a boy from a church-going family who had been bullied all his life because he couldn't talk properly because of his stutter. He had the face and the voice of an angel, and he had summoned up all his courage to enter the competition. When we first started the show, I dreamed about finding the modern-day equivalent of David Cassidy, and that's what I believed Gareth was. I was so blinkered at this point I couldn't even think of any other person winning. In fact, I did a bit of soul-searching; I worried that my bias towards Gareth was somehow wrong. But the more I thought about it, the more I decided that I was entitled to have a favourite. I was not only a judge, but also the record label of the eventual winner. Not to admit that I liked one singer more than another would be lying. Of course you have favourites. The only problem here is what happens if the one you support doesn't win, and the actual winner decides they don't like you because you supported the opposition.

Judging the Judges

Pete Waterman

When I went off to America to do American Idol, *Pete decided to do* Popstars: The Rivals, *a variation on the original show that pitted two bands against one another. In fact, Pete and I were both courted to do the show, but I couldn't do it. More to the point, I wouldn't do it. I listened to what they had to say, because I'll attend any meeting where I'm offered a job, but it seemed to me like it was an idea too close to* Pop Idol. *I said to Pete that I thought the general public was going to get fed up with us very quickly. In the end, he decided to do the show anyway. During the run of* American Idol, *I had some of the tapes shipped out to Los Angeles, and I was amazed by the chemistry among the three judges – Pete, Louis Walsh and Geri Halliwell. Or rather, the lack of chemistry. It was painful to watch. Sometimes you put a group of people together and it works, as it did on* Pop Idol *or* American Idol. *Sometimes you put a group of people together and it just falls flat. I thought the show itself was good, and parts of it were very good, but it was painful to watch Pete who appeared to hate every minute of it. As a judge of talent, Pete is still one of the best in the world, because he's not sitting there as a record producer. He's sitting there as a true lover of music and talent – a fan. Neil Fox sits there as a DJ. Nicki sits there as a management representative. I sit there as an A&R man. Pete is the only one who sits there as a true music lover. That's why I desperately wanted him on the second series; if he hadn't done it, I wouldn't have done it. I rely on Pete a lot during the show, and I also think he's one of the funniest people on television ever. Unintentionally, of course. He's so illogical, he gets so excited and emotional that he's wonderful to watch. Pete is TV gold.*

Neil Fox

Neil Fox is somebody who's always great fun to have on a show. I think Neil sometimes found it offensive when we described him as cheesy. But he is. He is corny and prattles on and can't contain his enthusiasm, and that's why I love him. That's why the public loves him. I don't want a Radio One DJ like Steve Lemacq, who arguably might bore some viewers to tears. Funnily enough, Neil has had quite a boost from the show, because people are getting fed up with the overly proper attitude of other DJs. They're starting to turn against people who take music so seriously, who wring it dry of any fun. Neil is a far better option.

Nicki Chapman

Having known Nicki for years from working together at BMG, I was gutted when she and the head of promotions left BMG to start their own company. They were a great team and very difficult to replace. Nicki was a solid presence the first time, good at balancing the more critical members of the panel and the more enthusiastic, but this time around she's much better. As we have started to judge the contestants on the second series she has made a number of comments about performances – about timing, about nuance – that have been 100 per cent right. She now has a bigger role after the first series, and I think that she's achieved that by becoming more technical, which is better for her.

Dear Simon,

Why don't you have a phone line for people to vote for the judge they hate most to be kicked off Popldol.

You can be assured of my vote.

Kind regards
Mr B

It was just before Christmas when the finalists assembled for the first of the 'Top Ten' shows: according to the format, the public would vote one contestant off each week until, nine weeks later, a Pop Idol was crowned.

Just before the first live show, Rik Waller lost his voice. Finally, proof that there was a God. I felt Rik had become more and more of a problem as his ego increased in size, and when he was told, on doctor's orders, that he couldn't enter the competition, he asked for time off. He was given a free pass for one week, but the executive producers and ITV decided that if he wasn't better by the following week, he'd be out.

On that first show, three of the contestants sang wonderfully (Gareth, Will and Zoe), while others lagged behind. When the public voted, the three who received the lowest number of votes sat together on the Sofa of Doom to await their fate. That first night, the unlucky ones were Laura, Jessica and Korben. Two hours later, after voting had closed, the results were announced, and Korben was no longer. I felt a bit bad for him, because he was technically one of the better singers on the show. But he didn't connect with the audience, and that's everything on *Pop Idol*. Korben was good-looking, had a great voice and looked the part. But he didn't have that impressive X Factor. One thing I do remember quite clearly from that night was thinking that this was not going to be the one-horse race I had thought it would be.

The next week, Rik still wasn't able to sing, so he was removed from the competition. That allowed us to give one of the other contestants from the previous round a free pass. The person picked was the one who had received the most votes – Darius. He gave the competition personality; love him or hate him, people talked about him, and that's vital for any talent competition. Sometimes he would literally make me cringe and other times I would feel proud for him that he had risen above all the ridicule. That night, he proved that he belonged in the competition, and rose to the occasion. The girls didn't do nearly as well: Jessica and Laura went back to the Sofa of Doom for the second consecutive week, where they were joined by Rosie Ribbons. This week, Jessica was voted off the show: nice girl, nice voice, goodbye. She later went on to represent Britain in the Eurovision Song Contest. She didn't win that either.

For the third week, the contestants had to pick songs from the vast catalogue of Burt Bacharach. Some did it better than others. Aaron Bayley went down into the bottom three, along with Laura and Rosie, and then learned that he had been eliminated. I would have liked to see him go further as he was one of the nicest contestants.

At that point, the fact that Laura was still hanging in there was something of a miracle – she had been on the verge of elimination three weeks in a row, and we started to wonder how much longer she could go on. Not much longer, as it turned out. She went out the very next week, when the theme was film songs. And the week after that took care of the other contestant who had been languishing in the bottom reaches, Rosie Ribbons. Rosie's departure was memorable in this regard: her performance on that show was one of the worst performances I have ever witnessed. This was strange, considering at one point Rosie had been one of the strong favourites to win the competition. The theme was ABBA songs, and she sang, 'The Winner Takes It All'. Well, maybe 'sing' isn't the right word. She murdered 'The Winner Takes It All'. She did everything but sing in key. We couldn't believe it. She just self-destructed and, to quote another ABBA song, this was her Waterloo. Rosie was out.

At this point we were down to five contestants: Gareth, Will, Hayley, Darius and Zoe. And something unbelievable occurred to me – Darius might win the competition! If you had said this to me nine months earlier it would have been insane. After *Popstars* Darius was a national joke; now he had a chance of winning the UK's biggest-ever talent competition. But he was singing well, he was charming, he had momentum. And the truth is, I wouldn't have minded.

The theme for the next show was big-band music. Zoe was very good, Will was brilliant, Gareth entertaining, Darius cheesy and Hayley a little bland. Hayley was voted out. I was pleased. The only girl left in the competition was Zoe. Suffice to say, no one expected her to stay around much longer.

OK, now it's time to talk about my trousers. It's quite amazing that I could spend half my life working quietly behind the scenes in the music business, before deciding to take the risk of appearing on national TV. Then, after spending 26 weeks on prime-time television, what was I going to be remembered for? The height of my trousers. Great!

It all started because of Ant and Dec. They never said a word to me about the height of my trousers, either on or off camera. In fact, nobody in my life had ever mentioned anything about my trousers, ever. Then, on one of the shows, Ant and Dec did a really funny impersonation of Pete and myself. I recognized Pete Waterman straight away, but I didn't know who the other guy was. Dec had these weird trousers on that came almost up to his nipples. Then I realized it was supposed to be me.

That was it. From that point on I was stuffed. I could not go anywhere in the country without somebody asking me why I wore my trousers so high. It got to the point that when I was introduced to people they never looked me in the eyes; they always looked straight down at my waistband. At that time I probably owned about 50 pairs of trousers. They were all Armani, and I suppose the fit was quite high. They were made that way. They couldn't change, but I could. The minute I arrived in the US to do *American Idol* I decided that I would never again tuck a T-shirt into my trousers.

I should point out, though, that the *Guardian* and the *Daily Telegraph* recently ran articles saying that high-waisted trousers were now back in fashion, thanks to me. They also reported that I was a 'stylish dresser'. So there.

Simon Says:
Looking Back at the Pop Idol Finalists

Korben He was the first one to go; while he had one of the best voices of the group, the public never warmed to him. His departure just proves how important personality is in this competition; if the public don't warm to your personality, you're out. Some people say that part of Korben's problem was that he was flamboyantly gay. I don't think that had anything to do with it. I would have liked him to have lasted a little longer because I thought he was a very good singer.

Jessica Garlick Jessica seemed to me to be in awe of Pete Waterman to the point where it was like watching some sort of pathetic schoolgirl with a horrible crush. Pete appeared to love it, of course. Jessica was a nice girl, very polite, probably a bit safe. That was about it.

Aaron Bayley I was really surprised that Aaron went out so early. I don't think there was a bad bone in that boy's body. He was the people's champion, but he realized very quickly that the music industry requires that you have a larger-than-life personality. All that people remember about Aaron was the fact that he was a nice bloke with a nice voice who drove a train. He couldn't cope with the big *Pop Idol* stage. He looked out of his depth. I liked Aaron very much. To me he is what this show is all about. One minute, you're driving the 8.15 from Crewe to London, and three months later, you're on stage in front of millions of people.

Laura Doherty How she survived so long in the competition, I'll never know. When I first met her in Glasgow I loved her to death. I thought she had a great personality, very unaffected. But when I saw her after she'd made the Top 10, she was, of all the girls, the one who I felt really did seem to believe her own hype a bit. She spent the longest in make-up and appeared to have the thinnest skin. And by the time she got through to the Top 10 she wasn't nearly as good. None of the judges championed her.

Rosie Ribbons Rosie was a real disappointment once we'd made the Top 10; she was the girl who I really did believe would be in the top two. I think she may have been having problems, although, if so, I don't know what they were. Plus, she came from a small town in Wales and I think her nerves did her in. Off camera, she was very warm, very friendly, very grateful for what we'd done for her, and I remember saying to her once, 'It's a real shame that you can't get over your personality as I know it on camera.' On camera she came over as a bit aloof, a bit cold, and when she sang Abba's 'The Winner Takes It All' it was just horrible to witness. She was somebody who could have been a real-life star with the right training, and there she was, crumbling in front of the nation.

Hayley Evetts Hayley just missed the mark for me. Good voice, good-looking but just not good enough. What Hayley didn't have is the right spark. I like her as a person, she's good fun off camera and unlike some of the others she's kept her 15 minutes of fame going for a long time. Will she have a hit record? Unlikely.

Zoe Birkett When Zoe went out it was probably the first time all of us got emotional, because Zoe had become sort of like the unofficial mascot of the show. She maintained her place in the competition through consistency. I think she was very nervous and had a huge bond with Gareth – people said they were like boyfriend and girlfriend, but they weren't. They were like brother and sister. They were both young, they were both shy and they were both dependent upon each other. Gareth, in particular, was devastated when she went out of the competition because he'd really lost his friend at that point. For my part, I thought it was the right decision. As Zoe got more and more help from the stylists and the make-up people, I felt she almost turned into a performing doll rather than what we had seen out on the road, which was raw talent with a little bit of an edge. It all got glossed over and I couldn't find anything exciting about her, which is why I never signed Zoe when the show was over.

Darius Danesh Darius was more prepared for *Pop Idol* than anybody else. He was the one who thought through his role on the show more completely than anyone else. And out of all the people on the show, he is, by far, the most charismatic. If I had to choose to go out to dinner or drinks with any one of the Top 10, he would be No. 1 on my list. This guy could turn on the charm, and when he met my mum at the final, she started acting like a 20-year-old. When he met my friends, they were in awe. I felt he was like a politician, so immaculate in his preparation that it came across like spontaneity. He became the real dark horse to win the competition. While everyone was talking about Will and Gareth, Darius was picking up vote after vote after vote each week. He had the whole of Scotland voting for him. I was absolutely thrilled that later on he got what he'd always wanted, a No. 1 record and a platinum album. To me, he was what *Pop Idol* stands for, which is that no matter how bad things are, if you've got the guts and you've got the determination, you can fulfil your dream. He wasn't the best singer by any means. Korben was a better singer than Darius and so was Aaron. But Darius has the X Factor. I think the fact that Darius was in our competition last year was one of the reasons the show did so well. He was great TV.

Gareth Gates From the moment I met Gareth in Manchester I wanted him to win. He looked good, had a great recording voice and, of course, his stammer made you root for him. He was also very ambitious. My feeling was that he would be great for my label and great for the show. If Gareth won it would be a fantastic story.

It's weird, this show. It draws you in. Why should I care who won the show? I had options on all of the Top 10. Win or lose, I was still able to give Gareth a recording contract. So why did I care? I don't know. I just wanted him to win. I actually felt quite protective about Gareth. He really is a very nice guy. When his singles went to No. 1 he would always send me a text message to say thank you.

There were a number of things that didn't help his chances of winning the show. Firstly, technically Will is a better singer than Gareth. Secondly, everyone thought Gareth was winning every one of the live shows. He wasn't, Will was. The week before the final it was reported that there was a tiny difference separating Will and Gareth, but Gareth was winning. It gave the impression that Gareth was more popular and therefore Will needed help. This was reflected in the bookmakers' odds that had Gareth as the clear favourite. I don't think I helped Gareth's cause. I was probably too sycophantic over him and this may have put people off voting for him. Anyway, I was a fan and, like everyone else on the night, I had a favourite.

Will Young People say that the confrontation between myself and Will in the early round caused a barrier. The truth is simpler: he knew that I wanted his main rival to win. I hardly spoke to Will at all throughout the competition. I complimented him many times on the show, but I was never able to get passionate about his performances in the same way as I did about Gareth's. Looking back, I can appreciate Will's position more. The only time we really got to talk was when I recorded the single 'Evergreen' with him because we had to have the three finalists record at the same time. Gareth and Darius had already recorded it, and Will came down to the studio and told me he didn't like the record. I asked him why, and he said, 'It's a pop record and it's not the sort of song I like.'

I took him upstairs to the studio, sat him down, and said, 'Look, Will, I think you're going to win this competition. This doesn't have to be the kind of music you're going to have to make for the rest of your life, but it has to be what you record now.'

In those brief minutes we spent together I liked him. I didn't think he was difficult, maybe a bit confused, but I liked and admired him for the fact that he was prepared to stand his own ground on something even before he'd won. After the competition Will decided to admit he was gay. I couldn't care less whether someone's straight or gay in this competition, it doesn't bother me in the slightest. For that matter, I think he could have announced it on the show and not suffered for it one iota. We live in the 21st century where no one gives a shit about stuff like that. Will is an amazing singer, an amazing talent, and that's what's important.

After almost two months of live shows, we were down to the final three: Will, Gareth and Darius. Looking back, I think Darius was resigned to leaving the show that night. Although Darius performed really well, he was voted out. I had very mixed feelings. While I was sad to see him go, I was also happy that he had done enough to achieve his dream. Darius was the comeback kid, from nothing – worse than nothing, if you count his abysmal *Popstars* audition. He had come in third out of 15,000 contestants. Once a national joke, he was now a thoroughly likeable bloke, a talented singer with a great personality. Afterwards, he thanked me for everything I'd done for him, and we parted on really, really good terms.

* * *

Then came the preparation for the finals. About five weeks earlier, we had sat down and had a strategy meeting to devise ways of making the competition as exciting as possible. We wanted to treat it like an electoral campaign with separate buses and different-coloured badges – and that's what happened. There had never been a pop campaign like this before. Forget Oasis and Blur, the whole country was talking about this. There was a clear north/ south divide, with the top half of the country rooting for Gareth and the lower half for Will. The hype was amazing.

The media were absolutely convinced Gareth was going to walk it, but I had a feeling in the back of my mind that Will would win. In fact, despite my personal preference, if I had had £1,000 to bet at the time I would have put it on Will a week before the final.

On the day of the final we turned up for rehearsals at 3 p.m. The two boys went through the songs they would be singing that night. At one point I turned round to Pete and said, 'Gareth's going to win this. He believes he can and Will has lost his spark.' He didn't answer. There was, generally, a lot of tension in the air that night. Nobody was smiling in rehearsals. We weren't having fun as we normally had done. We weren't taking the piss out of each other. It just didn't feel like a great night and I wanted it to be over with.

We took a break of about three hours, and when we

came back in for the live show, the place was absolutely electric. I had never felt anything like it, and it was obvious that the audience was an even split of passionate Gareth fans and passionate Will fans. When Will walked on for his first song, he was a different person from the one I'd seen in rehearsals, and the excitement from the audience was incredible. That's when I turned to Pete again and said, 'I was wrong earlier, Will is going to walk it.' It was a strange feeling for me that night. Sitting in the studio and feeling everyone going mental and knowing the winner's record would probably break all records was a huge buzz. And yet, I was miserable. Why? Because Gareth was being outsung and the fan in me was still unhappy. Incredible.

Gareth and Will sang their final two songs. The audience screamed equally loudly for both contestants. This was going to be a close vote. We had a three-hour break before the live result show and everyone was speculating. It was becoming clear that it would be impossible to predict the winner. The atmosphere was unbelievable backstage. You would have thought it was a general election. My phone would not stop ringing and members of the production staff were running in and out of my dressing room with updates on the vote. 'Gareth's in the lead', 'Will's taken over', 'Gareth leads by 1 per cent'. God, it was exciting. Then we were called back to the studio. The votes were in and we were going live in five minutes.

I desperately wanted to know the result before it was announced but no one would tell me. Out of the corner of my eye I saw the floor manager stop in his tracks. He had just been given the results on his headphone. 'You're kidding?' he said, into his mouthpiece.

'Who is it?' I asked. When he could see no one was watching he mouthed Will's name to me. I was actually gutted. It seems crazy now, 18 months later, but that's honestly how I felt that night.

Then I cast my mind back to nine months before, to the dinner at which Simon Fuller and I had discussed the show. We had said that the result would be as big as the O.J. Simpson verdict, and it was. What we had predicted had worked. Ant stood between Will and Gareth and then Will's name was announced. Cue pandemonium, cue fake smile from me. Will performed 'Evergreen', his first single, and I went back to my dressing room.

Five minutes later, Gareth came in with his mum and his dad, followed by Simon Fuller. He sat down and just burst into tears. It was very emotional. It was difficult for me to talk. Then Simon Fuller told Gareth that even though he had lost, he was going to be a star. We explained the plan to him: that he was going to have one day off, then a day recording 'Unchained Melody' and then a trip to Florida to shoot his video. I remember seeing a glimmer of a smile, and wondering if, maybe, he understood that as awful as he felt, he would be fine. Simon went up in my estimation at that moment. He lifted Gareth when he knew he was down. He wanted to ensure Gareth was happy before he spent time with Will.

After that, I met Will. I shook his hand and congratulated him, and he smiled and said, 'Thank you.' That was that. *Pop Idol* was over.

A few days later, I went out for dinner with Simon Fuller and we tried to sift through all the madness and process what had actually happened. Before we had even had time to recap, Simon raised the spectre of a second season, or an American version. I thought he was crazy. 'I've got to be honest with you,' I said. 'The way I feel at the moment, I'm not sure if I want to go through all this again.'

'Don't be such a drama queen,' he said. 'You've loved every second of it. The records are going to be big hits – America will love you.'

Eventually, we started talking about the business at hand, which was turning Will and Gareth's records into enormous hits. Will was taken care of, in a sense; he had recorded 'Evergreen' and we had huge orders for it already. We went over the Gareth plan in more detail, talked about his first single, his videos and so forth. We were determined to make successes of both of them. Just as important was to erase the record held by *Popstars*. The record that resulted from that series, 'Pure and Simple', held the record for the highest week-one sale for a debut artist, selling about 500,000 copies in the first week. Single sales were already in decline at this point, so we were both nervous that we were setting our sights too high.

The following week Will's single came out and sold 1.1 million copies in the first week. Three weeks later Gareth sold 950,000 in his first week. So we shattered the previous records with both the *Pop Idol* winner and the runner-up. Finally we could relax and reflect on our achievement.

The finalists' careers worked out rather well, all things considered. Sending Gareth to Florida was the best thing we ever did; it got him out the country during all the furore over Will, and it let him focus on his work. And the results were tremendous; his video for 'Unchained Melody' was one of the best pop videos I've ever been involved in.

For his part, Will came into BMG to meet everyone in the building and the buzz was tremendous. We had had everyone from Whitney Houston to Christina Aguilera visit us, but the day Will Young came in, not one person was off sick. That's when I started to regret that I didn't have a relationship with Will. He had always behaved in a very gentlemanly fashion with me. He was very gracious about me in his speech. He never spoke out of turn or complained about my treatment of him. I realized, in short, that I have a very serious character flaw. Well, nobody's perfect.

The third success story, of course, was Darius. I met him about two weeks after the final to discuss signing him to my label. He came over to my house and he was very charming, and while we both went through the motions of saying what we felt we should, neither of us had any passion about it at all. Eventually, he was brave enough to articulate what we were both thinking. 'The problem I have, Simon,' he said, 'is that I know I will always be third-best to Will and Gareth.' I made a feeble attempt to deny that, but, of course, he was right. Still, I gave him one excellent piece of career advice. I told him that what we should have made was a classic covers album, because when he sang a Tom Jones song during the live shows it was one of the highlights of *Pop Idol*. That advice didn't go down very well with him – he looked upon it as a strategy for making a quick buck. Darius wanted to write his own material, and that's exactly what he has done. He has had a No. 1 single and a platinum album. I'm proud of him and I respect his ambition, but let me be clear – no matter how well Darius has done on his own material, I would have sold more records my way, without a doubt.

The Best Pop Idol Performances

1. Gareth Gates, 'Unchained Melody'

This is one of my favourite songs of all time, so I'm slightly biased, but I can remember how I felt on the night. It was one of those magic moments when the artist and the song connect, and as a record executive you realize that you're going to have a No. 1 record. Gareth sang the song really well, and while he didn't outshine the Righteous Brothers – who could? – he made it his own. It went on to sell 1.5 million copies.

2. Will Young, 'Ain't No Sunshine'

During this performance, it dawned on me that Will was going to win this competition. For me, this was his defining moment, even more so than 'Light My Fire'. Will is a white soul singer; he's like a young Mick Hucknall, and as a result this was a perfect song for him. If I wasn't connected to the competition, I would have gone out and bought that single. I just loved it.

3. Darius Danesh, 'It's Not Unusual'

This was one of the cheesiest performances of one of the cheesiest songs of all time, and it was absolutely brilliant as a result. Darius wasn't taking himself too seriously, he had a lot of fun with it and suddenly he had what Tom Jones had – the ability to appeal to both kids and older people. This was the point at which the audience at home really forgave Darius for everything in the past – including his performances on *Popstars*. Great bloke, great personality and I just wish he had put that song out as a single, because, without doubt, it would have been a massive hit. I loved it.

The Worst Pop Idol Performances

1. Rosie Ribbons, 'The Winner Takes It All'

Rosie was one of my favourite singers in the Top 10, and 'The Winner Takes It All' is one of my favourite songs of all time. The combination should have been amazing; instead, the result was amazingly bad. I don't think Rosie sang one note in tune. Everything she had put into the competition was wiped out by this performance. That was the end of her.

2. Darius Danesh, 'Let's Face The Music And Dance'

Just awful. He sounded like some ghastly singer in a hotel lobby. If I had had a tomato in my pocket I would have thrown it at him – it was that bad. And just when you thought it couldn't get any worse, he turned to the camera and gave a little wink. Horrible, horrible, horrible. This is the song that caused a huge row between Pete Waterman and

myself. When I told Darius how much I hated his performance, Pete went mad, screaming at me and telling me I didn't
know what I was talking about.

3. Laura Doherty, 'Licensed To Kill'

Laura had all the tricks behind her that night: the set design
was superb, the lighting was great. Too bad she wasn't. I
thought she came onstage almost looking like someone from
The Addams Family and it only got worse from there.

Special Mention

Caroline Buckley, 'YMCA'

If any single performance summed up what this show is
about, it's this one. Absolutely bloody awful in every respect.
The greatest irony of all is that Caroline, having delivered the
worst performance of all time in any British TV song contest,
reprised her audition for the Grand Finale and ended up
making money singing in a Pizza Hut TV commercial with
me. Good for her.

Dear Mr Cowell,

Has it occurred to you that you may be
deaf?

Yours sincerely
Ms S

I had hardly been able to catch my breath before I got a phone call from Simon Fuller. 'Simon,' he said, 'Fox TV is going to run with *American Idol*.' They wanted me to be one of the judges so I had a decision to make. Simon had worked flat out to get a deal for us in the US and his hard work had paid off. Rupert Murdoch's daughter Elizabeth had persuaded her father to take *American Idol* seriously. His company owned the Fox network in America. I initially accepted and then decided I didn't want to do it after all. I told them I had changed my mind. The Americans were really pissed off. Luckily a friend of mine, Nicola Hill, persuaded me to change my mind and I reluctantly agreed.

At that point, all I knew for sure about the show was that it was going to be called *American Idol*. I also knew the identities of two of the other judges. One was a guy named Randy Jackson, whom I knew of in business circles as a very successful A&R guy with a great reputation. The third judge was Paula Abdul, whom I knew about from her pop career. The fourth judge was not yet selected. Nigel Lythgoe and Kenny Warwick would also be coming along to produce the American show.

My first morning in Los Angeles I was introduced to Randy Jackson over lunch, and it was one of those rare occasions in life when, within seconds, you find yourself totally at ease with another human being. The first thing that struck me about him was his personality. 'Sunny' didn't even begin to describe him – he could light up any room, no matter how large. He was familiar with the show, understood the concept, and, on top of all that, he was completely qualified. He had been a successful studio and touring bassist, and he had worked for years as an A&R man with artists like Mariah Carey. I didn't see any drawbacks to Randy. That didn't happen until later, when we were out on the road, and I came to realize that he was one of the worst name-droppers I'd come across. At that first meeting, though, I really warmed to him. The first round of auditions was scheduled for the very next day. 'You'll meet the rest of the crew tomorrow,' Nigel told me as he wrapped up the meeting. 'And of course you'll get to meet Paula.'

The next morning, horribly early, a car picked me up from my hotel and took me to the auditions. When I walked in, the first people I met were Ryan Seacrest and Brian Dunkleman, the two hosts. This, too, was a part of the formula lifted wholesale from the British version. But replicating Ant and Dec wasn't going to be so simple. Ant and Dec had been working together for years and they had honed their act very carefully. Brian and Ryan had just been thrown together – and, to make matters worse, they were polar opposites. Brian was a stand-up comic and, as a result, a cynic. And while it's true that many comedians aren't funny when they're offstage, Brian went one better – I didn't think he was funny onstage either. Plus, he didn't seem as if he wanted to do the show. Ryan, on the other hand, was totally different. He had started as an intern at a radio station in Atlanta and had moved quickly to Los Angeles where he became a popular DJ, and it was easy to see why. He was good-looking and enthusiastic, maybe too enthusiastic: I used to say that if he had a tail he would have wagged it. From the start, I was fairly certain that the partnership between the two hosts wouldn't survive, and that Brian was going to end up the casualty. That turned out to be the case, although I had to wait a whole year before it happened.

Brian Kadinski, the American executive producer, who I met along with Nigel and Kenny, completed the production triad. I liked Brian instantly, for his warmth and his sense of humour. Brian, along with Nigel was fixated on the issue of the fourth judge. 'Do we really need a fourth?' I asked him.

'Well,' he said, 'Fox is insisting on it because they've been told not to change the format.'

'Fine,' I said. 'When are we going to meet the first prospect?'

'He's right there,' Brian said, and pointed across the lobby.

I looked over and there was Mr Grey. Everything about this guy was grey: his hair, his skin colour, his clothes. When he came to sit with us, I learned that his personality was grey as well. I have since forgotten his name (no surprise), but I do remember that he worked as a magazine writer in New York, a very, very serious music writer. It was obvious to me that he would hate the show, and that anyone watching the show would hate him – and not in a good way.

'Have you seen the British version of the show?' I asked him.

'Yes,' he said. 'I've seen some tapes.'

'What did you think?'

'Well, I think I can add a different dimension to the panel, in that I believe that music is fundamentally an art form...'

As soon as this guy started to talk, I was overcome by the powerful urge to close my eyes and fall asleep. To me he was almost like human Valium. I excused myself and took Nigel off to the side.

'My God,' I said. 'This might be the most boring human being I have ever met in my entire life. If I have to go back and listen to him rattle on about art forms for another minute, I'll die. I'm going upstairs to have a shower. Call me when the other judge arrives.'

About a half-hour later, post-shower, Nigel called. 'We have the other candidate,' he said. His voice sounded strange. I went downstairs. This time, instead of Mr Grey, it was Mr... well, I'm not sure I can describe him. He was about 50 years old, and had hair down to his waist, or maybe even a little bit lower. He looked like an ageing roadie. Everyone around him wore an expression pitched midway between amusement and horror. The second I stepped towards this guy, he leapt up and gave me a vigorous two-handed handshake.

'Simon,' he said, 'I can't wait to start working with you. This is going to be fantastic.' I asked him to tell me a bit about himself, and it was as if I had launched a rocket. 'My main job is cartoon voices,' he said. 'But I do everything. I can DJ, I can sing, I'm a session singer, I do jingles. But my main thing, as I said, is cartoon voices.' He then proceeded to demonstrate with a medley: a little bit of Popeye, a bit of Mickey Mouse, some Minnie Mouse, some Goofy – he was a nightmare. 'Think of how much fun I'd be on the road,' he said. I glared at Nigel and he asked the guy to leave.

After he left, I sat down with Brian and Nigel. 'Please,' I said, 'let's just start off with three judges.' Brian reiterated that Fox was determined to keep the British formula intact. 'I understand that,' I said, 'but I would rather do it with just three people than work with guys like that.'

The other obstacle I had to overcome that first day, apart from my concern over Brian, was Paula Abdul. I remember quite clearly walking into the room and seeing her for the first time. 'Cute' was my first thought. 'Small' was my second. Of course, I was aware of Paula as a singer and a dancer, but I knew nothing about her as a person. She seemed nice enough, if reserved, and I sat down with her and Randy to briefly discuss the show. When it became clear that none of the judges Fox had selected was going to work out, we decided to stick with just the panel of three. The next morning, the judges went into the holding room to see the singers lining up to audition. They were clearing their throats, practising their scales, trying to remember the lyrics of their favourite songs. They were so excited, so full of hope. Little did they know what they were letting themselves in for. I don't think Paula knew, either.

* * *

The first singer to enter the *American Idol* judging session provided a historic moment in the history of American television – and in the history of abysmal singing. He sang and then, mercifully, stopped. He stood there, hopeful. Randy was the first to judge. 'Yeah,' he said, 'that was a little bit pitchy, but you were good, dog. I kind of liked it.'

Paula was equally noncommittal: 'I loved your audition and I admire your spirit,' she said. 'I don't know if it's quite the voice we're looking for, but I really like you.'

I cleared my throat. I had seen this kind of audition a million times on *Pop Idol*, and, of course, wasn't impressed. 'I think that we have to tell the truth here, which is that this singer is just awful. Not only do you look terrible, but you sound terrible. You're never going to be a pop star in a million years.' There was an eerie silence in the room.

After the contestant skulked off, Paula turned to face me. 'What did you just say?' she said.

'I just told him what I thought.'

'You can't talk to people like that,' she said.

'Yes, I can,' I said. 'In fact, I just did.'

'But this is America.'

'Yes. And?'

'And he's just a kid.'

'A kid who happens to sing terribly.'

'Are you going to keep doing this?' she said. 'He wasn't that bad.' She was more stubborn than I had expected.

'Paula,' I said, speaking slowly, 'he was that bad. And if they're really awful, then I believe we've got to tell them the truth. This is what I do. I'm not doing it to be rude, but I'm the record company here, and he was terrible.'

She stopped then, but the next singer was just as bad, and got a similar reaction and the one after that was even worse. It was carnage, and Paula was open-mouthed with horror.

After about an hour, I called Nigel and Kenny outside for a smoke and a talk. 'I think Paula is going to walk,' I said. 'I can just tell she hates this show. She hates me, certainly. And she doesn't want to be associated with something like this. I get the feeling she's too sweet.'

Nigel didn't disagree. 'But let's keep moving forward,' he said. 'Let's make it to lunchtime, at least, and then we'll see how she feels.'

The morning rolled along, but by then the contestants coming in had started to hear about the tone of the auditions from the contestants going out, and they were becoming a bit more combative. After we broke for lunch, I went to talk to Paula, as Nigel had suggested, and I found her backstage, sobbing her eyes out. 'Simon,' she said, 'I can't stay on this show. I didn't realize it was like this. This is terrible.'

'Look, Paula,' I said. 'We're not being vicious on purpose. But you and I know what the music industry is like, and we have promised the American audience that we're going to portray it honestly. You're out there because you're sweet, and I'm out there because I'm not. It's about striking a balance.' It didn't make a dent in her misery. For the rest of the afternoon, she was in pieces.

What was interesting after the first day was how completely it eradicated my anxieties about any differences between talent in Britain and America. In short, there was no difference. Just like back home, 90 per cent of the people were awful and 10 per cent were good. Since 100 per cent of the contestants believed that they were somehow destined to be big stars, that meant that 90 per cent were deluded. It was an epidemic.

However, there are some differences between the UK and the US contestants. The main difference is that in the US they really fight back. For example, there was a girl named Tamika who auditioned in Los Angeles. She wasn't very good, and we told her. In response, she told us, also in no uncertain terms, that she disagreed with us. She went crazy. She told us that we were stupid, and that she would prove us wrong. I loved her for that. Auditions are a very difficult, very one-sided process, and nine times out of ten, when you tell a contestant that he or she has no talent, they'll just thank you and slink out of the room. That's why I always encourage them to speak their minds. It's their only chance, and now and again they'll say something that will strike a chord with the judges, or even with the public. In Tamika's case, we aired her audition, and she became something of a folk hero for standing up to us, just as Will had been in *Pop Idol*.

The talent in L.A. was OK, but not amazing. There was one interesting girl called Tiffany Montgomery. She was a beautiful girl with an original vocal style, and we put her through, but she was extremely quiet and reserved. I thought her shyness would be a major problem, but Paula saw some potential for stardom in her, and decided to mentor her. That was very nice of Paula, but it had an unforeseen effect: Tiffany became so confident and so convinced of her own abilities that she became a pain in the ass. She changed her name to Ryan Starr, for starters, which is how she was known for the rest of the *American Idol* experience, and her attitude in later phases of the competition left something to be desired. If she was the cream of the crop in Los Angeles, I was worried. This was America, a huge country with a wonderful tradition of superb singers, and the best I had seen was a shy little girl with an OK voice and an identity crisis. 'Bloody hell,' I thought. 'I hope the rest of

America's better than this.' Seattle was a disappointment, so was Chicago.

When we got to New York, we encountered Milk, the Clark Kent lookalike who sang a version of Neil Diamond's 'Sweet Caroline' that was interspersed with Vietnam war footage. He did his routine, which was little more than a joke, and, when he finished, I turned to Randy, expecting him to be as thoroughly disgusted as I was. Instead, he said he quite liked him. I was furious. 'Fine,' I said, 'the two of you can judge without me.' I stood up and walked off.

Randy, for some reason, followed my lead and walked off as well. That left Paula on her own, and suddenly Randy and I realized that there was a slim chance that she might put him through to the next round. We ran back and dragged Milk out by his legs.

After lunch, Nigel and I returned to the auditions and heard a terrible wailing sound coming from the makeup room. It was Paula, crazed. 'I can't believe that you're letting them make me look like a fool,' Paula said to Nigel as we entered.

'What do you mean?' Nigel said.

Between sobs and gasps, Paula noticed me standing there in the doorway. 'How could you leave me alone and then come back in and undermine me?' she said. 'I need to be able to make the right decisions, but no one lets me make any decisions.'

Nigel explained that we couldn't let her put Milk through for her own sake, that it would have hurt her credibility. 'But we have put funny people through before,' she said.

'Yes,' Nigel said slowly, 'but he went too far.' He got through to her eventually, but the producers decided that Paula should take the rest of the afternoon off to clear her head. That was fine with me and fine with Randy. We went back into the audition room and carried on. Then, at some point, in the midst of somebody murdering a Stevie Wonder or Whitney Houston song, Paula reappeared. At that point, I really thought the entire show was in jeopardy. The tension was unbelievable, the bad feeling was so strong, that I didn't know how we could continue together.

The second day in New York, things eased up a bit, mostly because of Justin Guarini, who just came in and blew us all away. He was attractive, charming, with a good if not great voice, and he knew how to present himself. More to the point, he knew how to target Paula, who seemed to me to be almost instantly besotted with him. He appeared to turn her to jelly. At that point, I thought he might win the whole competition.

On the flight to Atlanta the next morning, the tension between Paula and me was horrific. I remember offering Paula an ice cream in the airport and receiving a terse reply delivered through gritted teeth. We travelled in silence. The following day we started the auditions, and that afternoon it all blew up. A contestant came in who I felt could hardly sing a note in tune. 'You've got prospects,' Paula said. 'With a few singing lessons, I think you could do well.'

I turned to Paula and said, 'I think you're patronizing this guy. If this was a hundred-metre sprint where you had to run it in 11 seconds to be competitive, he would take five hours. He is so far off the mark, he could take a thousand singing lessons and never be able to do any better than he's doing now. He's wasting his life.'

Paula turned to me, and I have never seen her look so furious. 'I'm not patronizing him!' she spat back.

'Yes, you are,' I replied.

When the contestant walked out of the room, Paula quickly followed.

That night, all of us met in Nigel's suite. Both producers, both hosts and all three judges. I didn't have high hopes for fixing things, but I told Paula to lighten up. The disagreements weren't personal, I explained, or shouldn't have been. We were judging talent. If Paula wanted to go on being too nice, or what I perceived as too nice, that was her right, but I was going to tell her what I thought of her opinion on camera. And if she disagreed with me or with Randy, she should hold her ground. We weren't actors. We were, essentially, on-screen A&R people who owed it to the audience and the contestants to be brutally honest.

For the first time in the whole process, Paula surprised me. 'OK,' she said. 'Now it's clear.' And from that moment on, although she lost her composure now and again, she was much calmer and more confident.

During a long and gruelling process like the *American Idol* auditions, nothing is more demoralizing than a bad set of contestants. And nothing is more invigorating than seeing a real talent emerge. Which is what happened on the second day in Atlanta. The morning went fairly well; we saw RJ Helton and EJay Day, both of whom would be Top 10 contestants, and some others who were good but not great. Then Tamyra Gray walked in and delivered one of the best auditions I've ever heard. Not one of the best *American Idol* auditions, but one of the best auditions, full stop. To me she was the complete package: she was smart, she was attractive, she had a beautiful voice, she had a calmness about her and she had presence. It was my first opportunity to give effusive praise, and I gave it. 'We're looking for the X Factor,' I said, 'but you have the Z Factor, because you go beyond X. You are to me what this competition's all about.'

Atlanta was also where I had a very bizarre conversation.

One of the junior producers came up to me on the second day and handed me a piece of paper. 'What is this?' I said.

'Well,' he said, 'the crew and I have written some more put-downs for you.' I was confused and said so.

'Put-downs,' he said. 'You know: insults. Someone writes your lines, don't they?'

'No,' I said.

'So you write them yourself?'

'They're not written,' I said. 'What I say is what I'm thinking.' This really surprised him.

He asked if I was sure I didn't want to take a look at the list.

'I am more than sure,' I said, 'because it's a script, and this has to be unscripted to work properly. I don't want to put myself in the position of reading what you've written, maybe liking it, and then changing what I do so I can say one of your clever lines.' He took his list and went back to his friends. Maybe they eventually got some use out of them somewhere else.

Texas was our next stop. We stayed in Dallas in a hotel the size of London. The talent was so-so. We did see one girl who was funny and had a good voice. Her name was Kelly Clarkson. After Dallas, Miami. And then the auditions were over.

We were all happy when we finally made it through the process. We were all certain that the show would be a big hit. But overall, I was slightly disappointed. In my mind, there were only two front-runners, Justin and Tamyra, and I would have been happy if either of them went on to win. I thought that Tamyra had a real chance to go on to be an international star.

I flew back to London to resume my normal life, and within about a week the auditions had faded from my memory. One afternoon, the phone rang. It was one of the American executive producers. 'It's a hit,' he said.

'What is?' I asked.

'The show, Simon. It aired last night and the ratings were fantastic. I've got 50 radio stations that want to talk to you.'

'About what?'

'About you.'

'When?'

'Right now.'

Half an hour later, I was on the phone with a seemingly endless series of radio DJs, all of whom were saying the same thing. 'Simon, the show's fantastic. We love your honesty. We can't believe how bad some of these singers are.'

'Wow,' I thought. 'They actually like me.' But I could sense there and then that the show was going to be huge.

After that first night when *American Idol* debuted, it just got bigger and bigger. I had to go back to the States, then start filming the final set of shows, what we called 'the heats'. At the airport the security guard stopped me. 'I'm afraid we may have a problem with you coming into our country, Mr Cowell.'

'Is there a problem with my visa?' I said.

'No,' he said. 'I watched *American Idol* last night.' Then he burst out laughing. When I got to the arrivals lounge, people were screaming my name and pointing. I think I may have heard some boos as well.

As the show progressed – with Paula and I still at each others' throats on a regular basis – we saw our field narrow from 100 to 50, and then to ten. My first thoughts on the Top 10 were not charitable ones. As a record label executive, there were still only two people who interested me at all, Tamyra Gray and Justin Guarini. Only two, that is, until we did the first live show and a girl named Kelly Clarkson walked out and opened her mouth. We had seen her in Dallas, Texas, where she hadn't impressed us as anything special: nice enough girl, good voice, good sense of humour. But when she sang live, I turned to Randy with my eyes wide and said to him that I thought she was going to walk this competition.

Randy just smiled an enormous smile and said, 'This time you're right.' Right at that moment, I started dreaming of a Kelly–Tamyra final. It would be just like Will and Gareth, only two girls. It would be perfect.

The popularity of the show had taken all of us by surprise, and in Paula's case it resulted in her reverting to her earlier diva state. Her entourage grew to at least a dozen people, and she grew happier and more confident. But there was an unforeseen consequence of her renewed confidence. During rehearsals one afternoon I heard a rumour that Paula had hired a scriptwriter to help her to take me on. I didn't believe it, but, sure enough, during the show, Paula turned to me after some comment and delivered this classic: 'Your father must have breast-fed you as a child.'

'What?' I was confused, along with everyone else in the studio.

She went on: 'The only high you'll ever get is if you smoke your own T-shirt.'

Unfortunately for her, she appeared to have somehow managed to hire what I felt was one of the worst comedy writers in Los Angeles. I had no response – what could you say to something that idiotic? But Paula looked like the cat who got the cream, because she felt she had managed to get one over on me. The next day, the Fox executives called us in and asked what the hell was happening.

'Well,' Paula said, 'Simon's so rude to me that I need to be able to answer him back.' I agreed, but I told her she didn't need any help, at which point she promptly denied hiring anyone to help her. I rolled my eyes, as I frequently did when she spoke. 'See?' she said. 'That's the kind of rudeness I'm talking about.'

Everything was going extremely well as the first season drew to a close, and I was sure we were going to have the Kelly–Tamyra finale I had dreamed of. I had even spoken to Fox about designing posters that depicted the last episode as a big boxing match, an Ali–Frazier scenario. Then, when it was down to four, Tamyra Gray gave the two worst performances she had given during the show's entire run. She looked nervous and sounded only mediocre. Nikki McKibbin – a Pat Benatar type who couldn't really sing a note but had a rebelliousness that appealed to the audience – followed her and gave the performance of her life. I still felt it wouldn't matter because Tamyra had been so consistent throughout. We opened up voting, closed the polls and went home. The next night, I was prepared to say something vaguely sincere to Nikki about how she had improved. Then Ryan opened and read the results: Tamyra was out of the competition.

I'll never forget it. I was horrified; I just couldn't believe it. I thought it was the wrong decision. Paula was devastated, Randy was devastated. Even Nikki, to her credit, was downcast because she knew she didn't deserve to be in that group and she had absolutely no chance of making the final.

The next week on the show, the energy levels were still low. Tamyra's departure had shocked the remaining contestants, and Justin and Kelly gave lacklustre performances. They were coasting. Nikki was voted off, as we all knew she would be, and suddenly we had our finalists: Justin and Kelly. I was disappointed, still thinking about what might have been if Tamyra and Kelly had been facing off.

The final episode was a two-part show spread over two nights: the performances and then the results. The three judges turned up at the Kodak Theatre only to be told by Nigel Lythgoe that we wouldn't be sitting in the normal judges' row. Instead, they were moving us to the absolute top of the theatre, so high up that we would look like tiny pinpricks. I thought it was stupid. We had been a part of the show throughout, and on the final night we weren't even allowed to speak. Backstage, Justin looked resigned, and Kelly looked as if she was rehearsing an acceptance speech. She was glowing. Justin came out first, sang poorly and Kelly came out and clinched the victory. To say it was one-sided is an understatement. It was anticlimactic from an artistic point of view. The irony is that I believe we – the judges – would have added to the drama that night. The performances without the critique didn't work, and I think we would have heightened the appeal of the show.

The following night was the results show. Now this is the big difference between the UK and US show. America does glitzy events better than any other country. It was like the Oscars, with a long red carpet, searchlights in the air, thousands of people lining the streets, and more than one hundred film crews. It made me smile to think back to the finale of *Pop Idol,* at Fountain Studios in north London. I remembered standing outside in the freezing cold as rain poured down on nine fans, one TV crew and half a dozen umbrellas. That night, as *American Idol* ended, I saw clearly what was so American about it: it was the scope, the excitement, the glamour. And the fact that there were 23 million people watching.

Finally, it came to the moment we had all been waiting for, or pretending to wait for. When Ryan announced that Kelly had won, I wanted only one thing to happen. I wanted Justin to show some disappointment or competitive spirit. He didn't. Instead, he jumped for bloody joy. That made no sense to me. This was a winner's competition, and it stood to reason that the person who lost would be, at least for a moment, unhappy. At least Kelly had the intelligence to look slightly surprised even though she obviously knew the victory was hers.

So in the end, why did Kelly win? I remember that Pete Waterman once made a prediction about *Pop Idol*. 'The winner won't be the flashy, controversial, good-looking showboater,' he said. 'It will be the person sitting quietly at the back of the room who's got the talent, and who knows they've got the talent, who will win this competition.' That's exactly what happened with Kelly. She was not on the radar until she made the Top 10, and that's when she came into her own.

Kelly also knew that singing was only part of the competition, and that the way she acted when she wasn't singing was just as important. Whenever the contestants would say goodbye to a departing singer, and start crying, she would be right there in the middle of it all. When one of us complimented her onstage, she had this little trick of looking humble. Oddly, I didn't get to know her very well during the competition. One afternoon, when there were about five contestants left, I tried to talk to her. I was having a cigarette and she was on her mobile phone, and I walked over and said, 'Kelly, I think you're going to do great in this competition, and I'm curious to know what kind of music you like personally.' She thanked me but said that she didn't feel comfortable talking to me because I was a judge. I thought it was a bit strange, but it also showed me how determined she was to stay focused. As it turned out, she was unquestionably the right person to win. We needed somebody who had the potential to be a big star both in America and around the globe, someone who was focused, who was talented, and who was a hard worker in every respect. Since the show, I've seen her confidence grow. Now, when you bump into Kelly Clarkson, you know that you're in the presence of a star.

Of course, before we could close the book on the first season, there was one absolutely crucial thing left to do. Without a hit single, the entire show meant nothing. I had learned that on *Pop Idol*, and we were about to test the theory again. Unfortunately the singles market in America was on its knees.

Simon put eighties singer-turned-songwriter Cathy Dennis together with a group of well-known American writers and the result was a very good song called 'Before Your Love'. Simon and I decided to make a double A side single with the winner. I had put one of the writers of Will's 'Evergreen', Jurgen Elofson, together with a talented friend of mine, John Reid, and they wrote a song called 'A Moment Like This'.

RCA sent Kelly's single out to radio stations a few weeks after the show had ended, and it sneaked into the lower reaches of the charts: Top 100, but nothing spectacular. Then it went on sale, and within the week it had jumped all the way to No. 1 – one of the biggest jumps in *Billboard* chart history. It went on to sell more than a million copies. For Simon Fuller and me, this was the moment when we could finally relax. If the single had stiffed after six months of hard work on the television series, we would have lost a tremendous amount of credibility for future seasons. We had to prove to the people who were watching that *American Idol* wasn't just a talent show, but the gateway to a real career.

It also had an impact on my career. As a record executive based in England, I was trained to think of America as the ultimate market: British music executives are always trying to succeed in the States with British artists. When I started as a judge on *American Idol*, I thought we may as Brits, succeed with American artists. When I first sat down with RCA Records at the beginning of the process and told them that they could sell a million singles by the winner of the competition, they looked at me as if I was out of my mind. So with Kelly's record sitting at the top of the charts, and with the reputation of the show secured – and my own reputation improved – I was finally able to turn my attention to the second season of the show. I had agreed to judge one more season of *American Idol* on the night of the final. Fox wanted the second series on air within five months – which meant auditions would begin almost straight away.

* * *

In the six weeks or so between the end of the first season of *American Idol* and the start of the second, the show was everywhere. America couldn't get enough of it. Kelly and Justin were stars. Even Paula, Randy and I were on magazine covers. The second season brought two other changes, one good and the other bad. The good news was that Brian Dunkleman wasn't coming back, which meant that Ryan would be the only host.

As we set out on the road for the auditions, the first person to catch our eye was Frenchie Davis, a big black woman with her hair dyed blonde who auditioned in New York. She was calm and serene but had a little smile on her face, as if she knew something that we didn't. Which she did. She knew that she could sing, and the second she opened her mouth we knew it, too. She was absolutely stunning, and the three of us turned to one another and said this girl's going to win the competition. She was that good. Frenchie told us that that she had made it to the auditions only because her college had bankrolled her trip. She had people who believed in her, and she believed in herself as well; when we told her she was coming through to the next round, she didn't even blink. She knew what she had.

I thought Frenchie was an interesting addition to the competition: she was a big girl, at least 20 stone, and she seemed to come from an earlier era, the late-disco period that produced the Weather Girls, Jocelyn Brown and other big, brassy divas. At that point, it occurred to me that the second season might be considerably different from the first, and that was an exciting notion. Frenchie, however, had a secret.

In New York, I also started to notice that the first season had distorted the contestants' view of the show and the judges, and that the distorted view was taking a toll on their performances. The first time around, no one had heard of me or Randy, and they may or may not have known Paula, so when they walked into the room, they were able to remain confident. During the second-season auditions, however, contestants came into the room as if they were having an audience with the Pope. We decided that the three judges should walk into the holding room each morning and intro-duce ourselves, break the ice and explain the process. We told them to stand up for themselves. 'Don't take any shit,' we said. 'Give it back.'

And they did.

I hadn't seen Paula for a few weeks since she had kissed me goodbye at the first-season finale. She had been glad to see me at the second-season kickoff. But as the second season got under way, it was clear to me that we weren't going to get along any better this time round. Like so many artists, I felt Paula was a mix of arrogance and insecurity. It was clear that she was tense; in New York, I knew that the relationship between me and Paula wasn't going to be very good.

There was also the strange matter of her growth spurt. I remember sitting next to her thinking that something was strange, but that I couldn't quite put my finger on it. In New York I realized what it was. Paula was higher up than me and Randy. I glanced down and saw that she was sitting on about four cushions. Obviously, some genius had told her that the best way to feel more confident with me and Randy was to appear taller. When she went out to the bathroom, I got one of the runners to get me and Randy five cushions each. When she came back in, we were all on cushions, and Randy and I were towering over her again. We were ridiculously high up over the tables. This continued throughout the competition, as did my habit of lowering her chair when she was out of the room. So I was elated when I learned that she wouldn't be making the trip to Atlanta, the next city, because she had to work on a film. I had loved Atlanta the first time around, and I figured that I would love it even more without Paula there.

The auditions started the morning after we arrived in Atlanta, and the main thing I remember is Clay Aiken. As I said before, the talent the second year was different. We were getting less of the kind of singer that dominated the first season of *American Idol*, the bratty girls who had been onstage since they could walk and wanted nothing more than to be the next Christina Aguilera or Britney Spears. Instead, we were seeing talented people who wouldn't normally enter a talent competition, good amateurs rather than bad professionals. Frenchie was a perfect example.

We hadn't had a particularly great morning when Clay walked in. He was really odd. Awful hair, thick glasses, goofy teeth. He was just a geek through and through; I remember thinking that if we put him on the front cover of a teen magazine, we would go out of business. He was nice enough but a complete mess. Then he started singing, and all his flaws were forgotten. When he finished his audition, he stood there, pleased with himself, but he was very nervous. 'Well,' I said, 'you don't look like a Pop Idol, you have to admit.' He nodded. 'But, God, you're a really good singer,' I said. 'What do we do with you?'

'Put me through,' he said. So we did. Randy felt exactly the same way about Clay; we agreed that there was an aura about him, something unusual. He stuck in our minds, and that alone was a tremendous achievement – when you see a hundred singers a day, it's amazing if you can remember even a handful of them.

Another instant contender was Ruben Studdard, who came from Nashville, Tennessee. Ruben was a big guy, but, unlike a lot of other big guys or big girls, he didn't see this as a problem. Sometimes, overweight people come into the room as if their weight will be held against them. Some come in with a huge chip on their shoulder and seem almost embarrassed to be there. But Ruben was one of those people whose personality walked in even before he did, and when he sang we didn't think of him as a fat guy, just a great singer. He was like a throwback to Luther Vandross or Barry White, one of those singers we haven't seen in a while.

By the time we left, though we were only halfway through the auditions, I was feeling more confident about the talent pool. Frenchie and Ruben were superb; Clay was a dark horse; we had plenty of the usual polished girl singers; and all in all, an interesting battle was shaping up: image versus talent.

Austin, Texas, was a nightmare. It's a great little town but the auditions were terrible. We had people dressed up as lizards, wizards, Christmas trees complete with fairy lights, vegetables and Klingons from *Star Trek*. I was really pissed off.

'What's next?' I asked Kenny Warwick.

'Two brothers, rich family, hate their father, want to be rock stars and love Paula.' Whoopee!

'Meet the younger brother first; if you don't like him he says he can perform with his brother.'

In walked the first brother. When I asked his name he sort of grunted and looked down at the floor. 'Go and get your brother,' I muttered. I was fed up. The two brothers came back into the room and told us they were going to sing Paula's hit 'Straight Up'. They were terrible. I was trying to get Kenny's attention because I thought one of the brothers looked like Ant. I couldn't catch his eye. And then they went into this terrible dance routine. Hang on a minute. I'd seen that routine before. I couldn't believe it. Ant and bloody Dec were in Texas. They got me. They really did.

After a number of other stops, we made our way back to Los Angeles. By that time, I was absolutely exhausted. The only bright spot was that Paula and I, after arguing on the road, were getting along again – we were back in our houses instead of in hotels, and I think that helped defuse the tension.

The L.A. auditions were OK, and we put through a few more contestants who were good but not brilliant. In particular we met Josh Gracin, who from the start knew what his role was in the competition: the patriot. He was in the American military, representing the Marines, and he literally marched into the audition room, saluted us and stood to attention. His presence couldn't have been more perfectly tailored to the national climate at that time, and when he sang he was good enough to impress us with his talent.

* * *

When it was time to narrow the field from the regional winners to the final group, I noticed that we had more determined and focused contestants than the first year. We actually took over two hundred people back to Hollywood, and our job was to find 32 finalists. It was around this time that the field of contestants began to follow its own internal dynamic, and I noticed right away that Ruben was often the centre of attention. Whenever there was a group song, the other performers would stand in a ring around him. There was something instinctive about it, the same way that you could look at early 'N Sync performances and see that Justin Timberlake was the centre, or look at early Supremes performances and see that Diana Ross was the centre, even though neither of them was necessarily the strongest singer in their group. The X Factor affects the other performers just as it affects an audience, and people are often intuitively aware of a front-runner or a leader.

The first time we did *American Idol*, no one really understood how it differed from any other talent show or variety show. Unless a contestant went online and researched the British version – and very few did – they didn't know what they were getting themselves into. The second-year crop knew everything. They had watched as Kelly Clarkson was delivered from obscurity into stardom; they knew the format of the show, the level of the competition and the value of the prize. In the span of just one year, the naive amateurs had all disappeared and they had been replaced by hardened competitors. One or two were already very aware that personality would make a massive difference this year.

Even so, the field of finalists was pretty easy to determine. Some singers had talent and others – most of the others – hadn't. Any process like this is designed to nurture talent. If you're a good judge, you know that. And I am a very good judge. All the people we liked at this point weren't perfect by any stretch. They all had problems, either with their delivery, their song selection, their fashion sense or their confidence. We were looking for those with the greatest potential; the singers and performers who could be moulded and encouraged. Frenchie, Ruben, Clay – all of them had a talent, that was clear, and, most importantly, were unique in their own way. I was very excited about having a different kind of performer this year, and very keen to see how the voting public would react.

I flew back to the UK and then went to Barbados for three weeks over Christmas. After arriving back in the UK, I was due to fly out to Los Angeles to start the second show. And then I got a call that changed everything. It was Kenny Warwick. 'Simon, I've got some bad news. Nigel's had a heart attack.'

'Oh God', I replied. 'How bad is it?'

'We're not sure,' said Kenny, 'but he won't be coming back for the show.'

I couldn't believe it. Nigel and his wife had been in Barbados with me. Nigel was a heavy smoker and didn't know there were things called fruit and vegetables. His previous diet was meat and meat – combined with a stressful job, this was a recipe for disaster. For days it was a real worry. I stayed in contact with his wife and his son. Thank God he survived. And in true Nigel Lythgoe style he was back at work within three weeks. No one could stop him.

Just before the show began there was a media blitz to promote the opening night. There was a lot of cynicism about how well the second series would do. Most people said that, after ending the first series with 23 million viewers, we should be prepared for a little reduction in numbers. I was confident. I thought we had a better show this time. Part of my thinking came from the talent pool, which was a much more interesting mix, but part came from the fact that we were going to show more of the early auditions. I was sure that audiences would respond to that, because it showcased what's inherently funny about the industry – the egos, the delusions, the tantrums, and, of course, the singers who were horrendous but believed they were the Second Coming. People kind of shook their heads sadly when I raved about the new season, but I was right. The first episode attracted

29 million viewers, and for about a week my phone wouldn't stop ringing. At that point, the *American Idol* phenomenon was firmly in place. We were on magazine covers, on the evening news. The show was huge, and wherever we went, people knew our names.

Then I got a phone call from Nigel Lythgoe.

'Simon,' he said, 'we have a problem.' Frenchie Davis, one of the odds-on favourites, had posed for an adult website some years before. Now her pictures had been discovered, and Nigel and Kenny thought she might have to be removed from the show.

I thought it was a tough call. As a record executive, I would keep her in. But if I was in Fox's shoes, protecting a billion-dollar brand, I didn't think I would risk offending family sponsors. There were subtler issues at play as well: at the auditions Frenchie had made it quite clear that she was trying to improve her life, and I wondered if maybe we weren't sending the wrong message by kicking her out. To Fox's credit, they spent weeks agonizing over the decision. But in the end they decided that she would have to go. I felt disappointed for Frenchie, but in a way she had skipped to the end of the competition. Of that early group, she was hands down the most famous, the one contestant everyone had already heard about. She may have got more than she bargained for, but she withstood the controversy and ended up in New York City with a prime role in the musical *Rent*.

Our twelve finalists were a mixed bunch. The front-runners were Ruben Studdard, our 30-stone Barry White lookalike, Josh the Marine, and Clay Aiken, our computer geek, who was now in the middle of a massive makeover.

My pleasure in seeing the second live season finally get under way was tempered by the fact that the executive producers and Fox, at long last, had decided to give us a celebrity judge each week. We were now supposed to welcome a different celebrity on each show to help us comment on the contestants (hurrah!). I wasn't in favour of this idea at all. I understood why the network was doing it, but I felt it undermined our credibility and threw off our chemistry. It also, frankly, cut into our time. Because I'm not shy, I let my feelings be known in the press, and after that I ended up having a heated argument with one of the executive producers. 'If you think it's such a good idea,' I said, 'why don't you bring in a celebrity executive producer next week?' He didn't see the humour in it.

Our first celebrity judge was Lamont Dozier, the legendary Motown songwriter who, with his partners Brian and Eddie Holland, was responsible for countless hits recorded by Martha and the Vandellas ('Heat Wave'),

Marvin Gaye ('Can I Get A Witness'), The Four Tops ('Standing In The Shadows Of Love') and especially the Supremes (Holland–Dozier–Holland wrote ten Top 10 hits for the group, including 'Baby Love', 'Stop! In the Name of Love' and 'You Keep Me Hanging On'). That night, the kids were all singing Motown hits. The show was fairly uneventful, with the exception of Clay's ongoing transformation. That week, he had a new hairstyle and he had fixed his teeth. It was as if he were serving notice to the rest of the contestants – and the viewers – that he was determined to go all the way. For me, it didn't quite work, because in those early live shows he was beginning to perform like some ghastly Las Vegas cabaret act.

In the weeks that followed, our guest judges included the famous soul singer Gladys Knight – best known for her hit 'Midnight Train To Georgia' – who coined Ruben's nickname, the 'velvet teddy bear'; Olivia Newton-John, who was very flirtatious and asked me to dinner after the show; and Verdine White, one of the kings of seventies funk and soul, who played bass for Earth, Wind and Fire. Verdine was indisputably a musical hero for those of us old enough to remember Earth, Wind and Fire. Randy, a bassist before he was an A&R executive, was especially impressed – but he was also one of the strangest people I have ever met. He was extremely nice, but his pre-show ritual took him at least five hours, and included at least three bottles of aftershave. And his clothes were like a costume: skintight leather trousers and a white frilly shirt that looked like he'd got them out of a time machine.

On the fifth show, the theme was *Billboard* No. 1 hits, and the judge was my favourite celebrity judge, Lionel Richie. He had a fantastic sense of humour, was as smart as a whip and was as musically astute as anyone I had ever met. It was great fun to work with him. One of the kids – Rickey, I think, who would end up being voted off that night – sang one of Lionel's songs, and afterwards Lionel praised him by saying that he had sung it almost as well as the original. As soon as he finished, I said, 'Well, with respect, Lionel, I never particularly liked your original.' He looked over at me, and it took him about a millionth of a second to realize that I was joking. But the audience thought it was real, and he played along with it. And for weeks afterwards, he continued to play along when he appeared on talk shows, even though when I met him out, we joked about it. Soon the Lionel Richie insult took on a life of its own. Clive Davis, who runs RCA Records in America and is one of the true moguls of the record business, called me one day and complained about my treatment of Lionel. I tried to explain it to him, but Clive is very old-fashioned about respect and he wasn't very happy about it.

* * *

In the middle of the series, war broke out. The producers and the Fox executives were put in a very difficult situation, because we had a No. 1 show in America at a time when all entertainment suddenly seemed frivolous. A Fox executive called me to say that they weren't going to pull the show, but that they needed us to be slightly more stately, to tone down the comedy. A woman named Susan, who worked for FremantleMedia, came up with the brilliant idea of having the kids sing Lee Greenwood's country song, 'God Bless the USA'. To say that the song got a reaction was an understatement. It was an incredible moment. The kids were fully engaged in the performance and visibly moved by the lyrics, the audience was spellbound and even a usually cynical judge like myself was touched. The phones were ringing off the hook. It was so powerful that one of the Fox executives insisted upon another performance of the song that night. Prior to that, we had planned on releasing a single with the cast singing Burt Bacharach's 'What The World Needs Now Is Love'. We'd already recorded the song and it turned out very well, but after the tremendous response to the war show, we decided to release both singles.

At this point Ruben and Clay mania was spreading through the United States. America adored these two. I was beginning, however, to feel that Ruben and Clay were in a bit of a rut. The theme of that week was songs of Billy Joel. Ruben did a Barry White-style cover of 'Just The Way You Are', and I criticized him for the first time. I told him he was playing it safe and becoming one-dimensional as a result. There was a gasp from the audience, and Ruben himself visibly jerked back as if he were stung. I'm sure the other contestants loved it, because we had been so sycophantic to him by that point that I had almost run out of compliments.

After the show, Ruben said, 'Can I have a word with you, Simon?'

'Certainly,' I said. I didn't know what to expect.

We went off to the side, and he took a deep breath. 'You know,' he said, 'that was the best advice anyone has ever given me. You're absolutely right. I was falling into a trap here, and I'll think about what you said.' I was impressed that Ruben had the maturity to respond this way.

The next week, Neil Sedaka joined us, and well, there is only one Neil Sedaka. He spent about an hour preparing, jotting down notes during the rehearsals, and he came up with some of the most hilarious phrases I have ever heard, including the infamous 'you are ear-delicious'. That was Clay's night to shine: he sang a version of 'Solitaire', which had been a hit for the Carpenters, that was absolutely breathtaking. It was one of the highlights of the whole series. He had the audience in the palm of his hand. 'I think he's going to win,' I said to Paula, and she agreed.

That night Ruben got the shock of his life. On the results show the following night, Ruben somehow fell into the bottom two and teetered on the brink of elimination. We were all shocked by this development, though in the back of my mind I thought that maybe his coasting had caught up with him. I didn't want him to be eliminated, of course – I had flashbacks to Tamyra's early departure the year before. Or rather, I had been having flashbacks all along, and I had done my best not even to fantasize about a Ruben–Clay final, lest I jeopardize it as I had jeopardized the Kelly–Tamyra final the first year. Luckily, Ruben made it through.

Robin Gibb of the Bee Gees ended the run of celebrity judges the following week, when the four remaining contestants – Ruben, Clay, Josh Gracin and another girl named Kimberly Locke – all sang Bee Gees songs. That was my favourite week musically, although it started off on an embarrassing note. Some weekly magazine had run a huge feature about how much I hated the idea of the celebrity judges, which was true, and it seemed to put Robin off a bit, although I had nothing against him personally. In fact, I felt bad for him – his brother Maurice had just died. The songs, of course, were absolutely sensational; the Bee Gees have produced so much great work, from their early pop songs through to their disco classics. Josh the marine, in particular, sang brilliantly. Even though he picked the same song, 'To Love Somebody', as Clay, he held his own. Josh was eliminated; he didn't have the consistency to keep up with the others. But he had saved the best for last, and he went out with his dignity intact. The low point of the night – of the whole season, in fact, and maybe the low point in the history of filmed musical performances – was Clay's second appearance. He sang 'Grease' wearing a red leather jacket, and he had an unbelievably awful dance routine to go along with it. Everything about it was horrible. And everything he'd accomplished the week before with Neil Sedaka's 'Solitaire', which was stylish and sophisticated, was thrown away with just one performance. I still believe that it may have cost him the overall competition, because that performance was so awful that it was hard to get past it in your mind. The following week we had two guys, Ruben and Clay, and one girl, Kimberly Locke, competing for a place in the final. Kimberly had a great voice but looked like a librarian. She was out. We had got the final I wanted. Ruben vs Clay.

On the night of the final every radio station and newspaper wanted to do interviews with the judges and the contestants. I went down the hall to talk to Clay and Ruben, and both of them were extremely nervous. Ruben wasn't himself. He was sweating, he looked agitated and for the first time he looked scared. Clay was only slightly less anxious. I wished them both luck; I told them that it had been a pleasure working with the two of them, and that they should enjoy the fact that they were performing in front of millions of people. I don't think they heard a word I said.

Both contestants had to sing three songs that night, and the first two performances from each were fairly disappointing. I knew, the audience knew and both Ruben and Clay knew that, so far, their performances were disappointing. This was the climax to everything we had worked for – the final of *American Idol*. Where was the drama? Where was the wow factor? Now we were down to the third and final songs, and Ruben was to go first. The song he had chosen was 'Flying Without Wings', a song that had been a No. 1 hit for Westlife three years before.

Ruben walked out on the stage. I could see him steadying himself, aware that this was the last song he would sing in the competition. The audience was unusually quiet – they sensed that he could win or lose everything with this performance.

He started singing, and this was the Ruben we loved. You could see him lifting himself throughout the song, and when the gospel choir joined him at the end it was a spectacular moment. When he finished the auditorium exploded. Now there was only one more song to go.

Clay, the most ambitious and astute of the final 12, must have been in pieces. He knew Ruben had delivered a great performance. I knew he had chosen 'Bridge Over Troubled Water' for his last song, and I also knew what a difficult song this is to sing. When Clay walked out onto the stage that night, I saw his nerves for the first time. For once, he seemed unsure. He closed his eyes and sang the first line, and I could actually feel the hairs stand up on the back of my neck. It was incredible. When he finished the audience went crazy. Clay looked triumphant. At that moment, I would have bet my house on Clay Aiken becoming the next American Idol.

I bumped into Ruben and Clay minutes afterwards, just as we prepared for the media blitz. I looked at the two of them, and it was obvious that they both thought Clay had the victory sewn up. But at home later, watching the tapes, I changed my mind. Ruben's performance over the entire night was stronger. At any rate, it was too close to call.

The following day, as we were getting ready for the results show – a two-hour *American Idol* extravaganza – my house was total pandemonium. Phones were ringing off the hook, presents were arriving, people were running in and out. Terri was arranging everything: the whole world wanted tickets, and she ended up getting dressed in the limousine.

Two of the producers, Charles and David, had thought it would be a good idea for Paula and me to do some imaginary

love scene, because all season long the press had been speculating about whether we were having an affair. Freedom of
the press is a good thing, but this seemed ridiculous. At any
rate, we thought it would be funny to do a scene shot at my
house in which Paula and I were having dinner. It would end
with a kiss, and then I would wake up, as if from a dream, to
find Randy in my bed – at which point I would scream.
Wouldn't you? When it was shown, however, it was far more
graphic than I'd remembered. Paula was sucking cream off
her fingers in a very sexual manner, and was licking a straw-
berry. I looked behind me and caught Terri's gaze. She
wasn't amused.

Finally, there was total silence in the auditorium as Ryan
prepared to read out the winner. Was it Ruben? Was it Clay?
Was it Ruben? Was it Clay? It was Ruben, and the entire
theatre erupted in applause as Ruben stood there looking
utterly stunned. Clay had a sort of fake smile on his face; he
wasn't happy at all. The chaos consumed all of us. In fact, the
only thing I remember clearly was Ruben and Clay leaving
the auditorium on the way to the press tent. Ruben was
surrounded by about two dozen people. He was sweating
profusely and looked like he was on another planet. Clay,
who came next, had one press representative. 'My God,' I
thought, 'there's the difference between being the winner
and the runner-up.'

The second season had come to a close, and the ending had been better than I had ever imagined. Everything we had worked for – from my first discussions with Simon Fuller about *Pop Idol*, to Will and Gareth and the first *Pop Idol* finale, to our first steps entering the American market – had culminated in a spectacular finish that not only drew 50 million viewers – a staggering number – but would dominate all discussions of pop culture and the entertainment media in America for the foreseeable future. But it was time to get back to England.

I Don't Mean to Be Rude, But...
Young People Today

While I was away in Barbados I had a chance to relax and think about the state of the pop market. What was obvious was we were now living in a fame epidemic. There has never been a time when so many young people sought celebrity status. When I was at school and someone asked a question about what you wanted to be when you left school, most of the boys would say a train driver or a racing driver. Now the answer is famous. And who can blame them? Just about every magazine available portrays a lifestyle that looks great – David and Victoria, J. Lo and Ben, P. Diddy and whoever, all swept up in a world of private planes, luxury yachts, shopping on Rodeo Drive or Sloane Street. What a life. I would assume every teenager reading those magazines would think 'That could be me.' And this is what Pop Idol reflects. Anyone has a shot.

But my job is to point out to all the hopefuls the realistic chances of reaching that goal. Firstly, if you want that lifestyle you have to have talent. Secondly, you have to realize that you may actually have to work for it. My favourite experience on the show is the contestant who tells us 'I've given up everything for this. I've sacrificed a lot to live this dream.' 'How old are you?' I ask. '17,' they reply.

In other words, the show is an accurate representation of life today. Make me famous. Make me rich. I want it all. Now!

I wasn't even sure whether there was going to be a second
series of *Pop Idol*. The first series' finale had huge
ratings; something like 13 or 14 million people had tuned in
and we had nearly 10 million votes. But even when it was
fresh in my mind, I was reluctant to jump right back into it
for a second series.

After *American Idol*, the decision was even more compli-
cated. The massive success of that show led to a lucrative
contract for three more years, but that also cast my role on
the British series into doubt. I feared falling into a rut, or
becoming a professional judge, which would have been
tragic for two reasons. For starters, I have always got as much
pleasure from being behind the scenes. In fact, I probably
prefer it. And there's also the matter of my own credibility. I

didn't want to end up three seasons in with nothing interesting to say. You don't want to be this kind of horrible caricature who is always saying, 'You're dreadful...you're ghastly.'

Finally, in March 2003, I decided to sign on for another year of the UK show. This may sound a little worthy, but the main reason I returned was because of the gratitude and the obligation I felt to ITV. If they hadn't given us the support and the funding I wouldn't have got the deal with Fox, or sold all the records we have. It's still a well-paid job, don't get me wrong, but there's also a principle at stake.

I was back, but some others were gone. Nigel Lythgoe and Kenny Warwick, who had been executive producers of the first *Pop Idol*, had decided to stay out in the US and focus on *American Idol*. That meant that Richard Holloway, one of the executive producers on the first series, would oversee the whole series, along with Claire Horton. There were also a few minor format changes. After two seasons in America, for example, we found that the competition was greatly improved by the wildcard shows – which gave us the opportunity to bring back some of the more interesting talent and give them a second chance to make the Top 10. But essentially it was the same show. Objectively, that is. Subjectively, it couldn't have been more different. The first year, no one knew what to expect from the show. The public didn't know. The media didn't know. The second year, expectations were much greater. Audience expectations were greater, and even contestants' expectations were greater – the kids we saw for the auditions for the second series were significantly more driven and focused.

As we found out on the first day, the judges had also changed since the first series. It was the same four again but now we had all become TV personalities, and there was the temptation to play to the camera. If we had been able, during the first season, to sometimes forget that we were on television, during the second season it was impossible. There was one moment in the middle of the first day, in fact, where I thought that the whole panel wasn't working. The power dynamic had shifted, and it was almost as if the judges were performing for the kids rather than the other way around. I sat down with the producers at the end of the day and told them my concerns. Their reaction was to give it time.

They were absolutely right. It was a first-day problem. On the first day of any show you are conscious of the lights and cameras and the fact that you are on TV. By the second day, after listening to 160 wannabes who can't sing quite in time, you don't care. You just want them to leave the room.

What was most astonishing about the first day was how many terrible singers were turning up. I couldn't believe it. What amazed me even more was how deluded they were. People were coming in with some of the worst voices I've ever heard in my life, we were obviously telling them they were terrible and they were looking at me or Pete or whoever had just given it to them straight as if we were the crazy ones. One guy came in and I stopped him midway through the audition. 'Did you watch the first series?' I said.

'Yes.'

'Well, why are you here? You can't sing.'

His eyes widened in disbelief. 'You've got it wrong,' he said. 'I'm fantastic.' It occurred to me for a second that he was performing badly on purpose. Out of all the judges, I'm the one who usually spots those people. A bad singer who believes in himself has a different look in his eyes from that of a bad singer who comes in to make a mockery of the audition process – the latter often has a funny little smile, or a weird kind of bravado. The first season, it happened rarely, but the national awareness that *Pop Idol* was a surefire route to stardom may have encouraged a certain number of kids to come on and make fools of themselves on purpose. It is important to demonstrate on our show that, good or bad, they all genuinely believe they are the greatest.

Through the second season auditions, we started to see something similar to what we saw in America. The cities were the same – London, Manchester and Glasgow – but we were attracting a different kind of auditionee. Generally, they didn't have the stage school mentality. Rather, they were genuinely good singers who didn't have a great image. That set up a similar battle between image and talent that we had witnessed in America during the second series, which had made the second season much more interesting than the first, and, of course, better television.

The first few episodes of the second series, the audition shows, were just superb television. The way that Richard and Claire, the two producers, used music as a backdrop to tell the stories was brilliant.

After a three-week stint across the UK we brought back approximately 100 people to audition for us again in London. I was actually pleased with the standard this time around. We'd found a diverse bunch and I was particularly keen to see how our larger contestants would fare this time round. I'd got to the point where I was sick to death of seeing wave after wave of Atomic Kitten clones. All of these girls looked and sounded the same. I had a hunch that the public was getting tired of this as well.

The Criterion Theatre in London is where we decided who was going to make our final 50. What I noticed this year was the desire to make it through to the next round was much stronger this time. These kids really really wanted it. Each day we would have to let about 25 go and they were distraught.

One of these was Nicola Gates, Gareth's sister. Nicola had auditioned for us on series one and she nearly made the Top 100. I was surprised she had decided to give it another go. We saw her in Manchester and she had adopted a new name, Nicola J. She wasn't very good and wore a weird outfit, which consisted of one trouser leg tucked into her boot. I actually felt sorry for her and gave her another shot. In London, she didn't shine and she was out on the first day – she wasn't happy! In truth this should be the end of the line for her – I really don't think she will ever be good enough.

There were, however, quite a few others who did shine. Michelle, our big girl from Glasgow, was fantastic. She had a great attitude and nearly collapsed when she heard she'd made it through to the final 50.

Sam, one of my early favourites shone, Brian from Ireland emerged as an early favourite and two Scottish boys, and Kieran and Marc, were superb. We all really liked a sweet shy girl called Susanne but I was convinced her nerves would destroy her.

One contestant I couldn't agree on with the others was Chris. Foxy had nicknamed him the Vicar and all three of the other judges loved him. I didn't.

On the final day we had to eliminate 25 contestants to arrive at our final 50. And, yes, Pete threw a fit again. Every time the big contestants were mentioned he went nuts. But that's why I am so fond of Pete. He speaks his mind and he doesn't give a shit. We also got into a row over Tarek. I wanted him to make the final 50 but Pete didn't. I argued that there were only 15 or 20 out of the final 50 who I thought were good. I wanted to put somebody with personality into the final 50 rather than a bland nobody. I won, he went through. We had our 50 and we all felt that the heat shows would be interesting.

The heats took place at Teddington Studios. Each week 10 would perform and the public would vote two through to the finals. On week one Michelle was up against three strong candidates: Rebecca, a cute girl we had seen in London with a very sexy image, Chris, the Vicar and Jason, the grannies' favourite. Michelle outsang them all. Chris was actually very good, Rebecca was good and Jason was sweet. Michelle and Chris were voted through and the other two were distraught. At this stage no one was aware there was going to be a wild-card show and they thought this was the end of the road.

On our second show, Brian Ormond from Dublin was expected to walk it. On the night he was very good. Susanne Manning, who we all wanted to do well, blew it. She looked nervous and was under par. One girl who wasn't on our radar, Kirsty Gallagher, was superb and she won that night along with Brian, who came a close second. Overall the standard was fairly poor that night.

Week Three was our best so far. Kieran was favourite to win. As he came on stage I was surprised at how different he looked. But it didn't work. He'd lost his vulnerability and just looked strange to me. Vocally, it was his worst performance so far in the competition. And then Roxanne Cooper sang. Bloody hell, I thought, where did she come from? She was amazing. She sang Christina Aguilera's 'Beautiful'. She was stunning. Last up was Marc Dillon from Scotland. I'd found out that day that Marc had a bit of a past and had actually spent time in prison a few years ago. None of us expected him to beat Kieran. His audition was superb and he walked it. As soon as he finished singing he burst into tears. After we congratulated him he almost fell apart in the green room with Ant and Dec; he just couldn't stop crying. It was the emotion of singing well coupled with the stress of the media attention he had been receiving in Scotland over his past. That night, on the result show, Marc won – he cried again. I was delighted and Roxanne came second.

Week Four was a disaster. In my opinion no one shone. Kim, our mother of two, made it through with Leon who I was never a fan of. I left the show depressed that night.

Week Five was weird. I couldn't remember half of the contestants. Once again the standard wasn't great. We all rooted for Andy Scott-Lee, Mr Nice. His sister was in Steps and he had previously been signed to Sony with his two brothers as 3SL. I had actually been to one of their earlier showcases when they were trying to get a deal and I didn't think they were good enough.

Andy was OK on the night but we all hoped he'd make it through and of course he did with Mark Rhodes. I told Mark on the night that I didn't see his personality but he was very funny afterwards with Ant and Dec. Good value.

We announced the fact that this year there would be a wildcard show in which we could bring back eight people who hadn't made it through. It was pretty easy really. The clear favourites were Susanne, Sam, Jason and Kieran.

Susanne stole the show that night. We knew the public would vote her through and they did. It was up to us to decide who came second. In fact, for the first time we didn't deliberate. We awarded the contestants points. Sam came second. No one was unhappy about this and he was thrilled when we told him. My gut feeling at this point was that Susanne had made her mark on the competition and would be the one to beat. We had our Top 12.

Looking Back at the Pop Idol 2 Finalists

Michelle One of my favourites. A big girl with a huge voice. Michelle has a great personality and still can't believe she's in the Top 12. Michelle is a born entertainer and I can't help liking her.

Chris Not one of my favourites. You either love him or hate him. He's funny with a quirky personality. Sometimes it looks as if he doesn't know he's even there. It's weird. I have had people call me and say they think Chris is one of the best singers they have ever heard and others will say they can't stand his voice. The public seems to like him. His weakness is his inconsistency and awkwardness when performing.

Susanne Again, one of my favourites. She looks so vulnerable and the public has really taken to her. This will help her in the competition. She wasn't the best performer, but this girl can sing. Her strengths are her voice, her sweetness and a face made for TV. Her weakness is her awkwardness when performing and her nerves, which could still cripple her.

Roxanne A real born star in the making. She's funny and I've never heard anyone say a bad word about her. Once she finds the right style of song she's going to be a real contender. It still amazes me that she is only 16 years old. Her strengths are that she looks the part, has a great personality and when she's on form has an amazing voice. Her weakness is once again inconsistency.

Brian He could be a member of Westlife. A nice guy, nice voice but a little bland for me. He has been eliminated already perhaps because he chose the wrong song that week.

Mark Rhodes He is a bit of a dark horse. Mark has a very good voice and the more you get to see of him, the more you like him. He's funny and self-effacing. His strength is his voice and the character that's beginning to emerge. His weakness is he has a tendency to choose the wrong song. He's not the best performer either.

Kirsty Once again she has already been eliminated too. That was no surprise to me. I thought she chose a terrible song and just blew it. She seemed to want to win it so badly, I found it painful to witness. When Ant and Dec told her the verdict she collapsed on stage.

Kim Is she an undiscovered talent or a pub singer who got lucky? I'm not sure. I like Kim and I'm pleased she made the Top 12 but I am still a little sceptical. On the first live show she outsang Michelle but I think Michelle will do better than her. Her strengths are her voice, when she chooses the right song for her, and the underdog tag. Her weakness is she rarely looks like a star.

Marc Dillon Marc has also been eliminated. And I am actually very sorry about that because I think he had a great voice and a great character. When I heard 'Celebration', I couldn't believe it. I knew he'd made the wrong choice. He sounded and looked like an average Karaoke singer. And he's not. The song killed him. How ironic bearing in mind the title of the song.

Leon He went out in Week One. Leon's a nice kid but he was out of his depth. I don't think he likes me very much!

Andy I thought when he made it through he would be lucky to last two weeks. But Andy is becoming a bit of a revelation. He's actually starting to believe in himself and it shows. Andy looks like he could be there at the end. His strengths are his ability to choose good songs, which suit his voice, his looks and his modesty. His weakness is the fact that he's not the best singer in the competition.

Sam He was the second wildcard choice. Along with Andy he's our resident heartthrob. He's funny, charming and has a great voice when he finds the right song. His main strength is that he has a strong voice. He also comes over well in interviews as the cheeky little chap. His weakness is that his voice is bland when he chooses the wrong material.

Special Mention

Rachel Ifon She came to the Manchester auditions from Liverpool, where she worked in a Bingo hall. She told us that, and much, much more. She was absolutely hysterical; she could talk for England. I wouldn't say she had an especially strong voice, but she just lit up the room. If the show was called *Personality Idol*, I'd give her the prize now. I loved her – she should have her own TV show and be the next Cilla Black. On the night I thought she didn't sing a note in tune, but we still loved her. We decided to give her a chance and put her into the 50 because we all remembered this girl. When someone like Rachel comes in, who made us laugh and then talk about her afterwards, it's a refreshing change.

At the time of writing, I am going to stick my neck out and say who I think is going to win *Pop Idol 2*. Michelle. She had a bad first week but I have a hunch she could do it. And yes, if she does we'll sell a lot of records with her. I do think Susanne could give her a run for her money.

I Don't Mean to Be Rude, But...
We're Better than Fame Academy

Just as we finished the auditions for the second series, I got a phone call from Claudia Rosenkrantz early one morning to say that she had found out that the BBC's show, Fame Academy, *was going to go up against* Pop Idol. *She sounded a bit concerned. 'Don't worry about it,' I said. And I wasn't worried. But I do think that it's terrible that they're putting the two shows up against each other. It's so clearly a spoiler tactic. Which isn't to say that there's anything wrong with* Fame Academy, *I think they've found some good talent on their show; this girl Alex is a gem, a real find. The only problem I have with* Fame Academy *is that I find it a bit worthy.* Pop Idol *works because it's irreverent and bizarre and funny, because it's about the record business, and having worked in the music business for 25 years, I can tell you that it's probably the funniest business on earth. You can't be serious about it. The characters are just so ridiculous. Some people forget this. It's why* Top of the Pops *is in the mess it's in. I remember* Top of the Pops *in its heyday, when it had Peter Powell in a safari hat with people around him dressed as animals and dancing to 'The Lion Sleeps Tonight' by Tight Fit. It was tacky, maybe, but it was great fun to watch. When I watch* Top of the Pops *now, I don't find anything funny in it any more, unless it's the Cheeky Girls – but that's unintentionally funny. On* Pop Idol, *we're not taking ourselves too seriously. We're not saying that we're getting every-thing right. Our main job is to make an entertaining television show, which honestly reflects the pop music industry. If we ever get it totally right, though, no one will watch.*

Dear Simon,

I hate you but my sister likes you.

My mummy thinks you should shut up.

Best wishes
Darren (Aged 6)

PS can I have a signed photo.

Believe it or not, I'm often approached by young singers who ask me what they need to do to break into the music industry. I always start by giving people the same piece of advice: don't bother. Sometimes they laugh. Sometimes they shift uncomfortably. But I'm dead serious. In almost every case, 'Don't bother' is the wise course. The odds against succeeding are absolutely astronomical; in some ways, you would have better luck if you set your heart on being Prime Minister or played the lottery. If you look around and take the measure of every entertainer in every corner of the country, I think you'll see what I mean. Have you ever met a hotel bar singer who tells you, 'Yes, I entered the music business so I could end up singing in a hotel bar?'

But plenty of young singers don't listen to me when I tell them not to bother. They have drive and ambition, and they're convinced of their talent. Good for them. They have already passed the first test, which is to make sure that they have the stomach for this business. It's never an easy road, and even when you think you have made it, you can't rest. Any entertainment career requires ridiculous amounts of hard work and difficult sacrifices. Of course, the rewards, if you are lucky enough to enjoy them, are also huge, but getting there is almost impossible.

Pop music is particularly tricky. I like to tell young singers that if they are geniuses who can write songs like Elton John or the Beatles, fantastic – you can rest easy. Anyone who can write 'Sorry Seems To Be The Hardest Word' or 'Eleanor Rigby' will draw the attention of one of the hundreds of publishing companies out there. They'll snap you up within seconds. They are unique. But almost no one is as talented as Elton John or the Beatles. And if you're like most aspiring pop artists, you're primarily a performer. Pop acts are throwbacks in some ways; unlike modern rock bands, they tend not to write their own material. This means, of course, that a record company is investing in you as a performer, as a talent – they are banking on you having the charisma, the energy, the focus and the X Factor to be able to sell millions of records. You are the musical equivalent of Leonardo DiCaprio: you're talented, but you need writers and direction.

This faith isn't free, though. If a record company signs you up as a solo artist and commits to a deal, they will have to invest millions of pounds in you. No company is going to do that unless they see something really special about you. And if the first single doesn't perform, the game may be over. The investment is gone. I'm not saying that this is an ideal circumstance, but it is reality. Trying to launch a solo artist who doesn't write his or her own material is the hardest thing in the world.

With that said, there are some basic rules that all aspiring singers and entertainers should follow. These don't guarantee you success, but they will help you maximize your chances, and that's all you can ask for. Because truthfully, even with my expert advice in hand, you're going to need all the help you can get.

My Top 5 Classic Vocalists

Frank Sinatra

Bobby Hatfield of the Righteous Brothers

Bobby Darin

Tony Bennett

Ella Fitzgerald

Create a Platform

Pop artists don't appear out of thin air. Sometimes it seems like they do, but that's just skilful marketing and sleight of hand. The truth is that they all come from somewhere, and usually somewhere else within the entertainment industry. Without some pre-existing context, in fact, it is highly difficult to be signed by any record company executive who wants to keep his job longer than a week or two. One way to establish yourself and create a platform, obviously, is to place yourself in a band. This is a bitter pill for many aspiring stars to swallow; most young entertainers have huge egos, and they all want to be the name above the title, the marquee star. But take it from me – it's nearly impossible to launch an unknown into a bona fide solo career. That's one of the reasons why *Pop Idol* was born. But there's an ironic by-product of the phenomenal successes. Because of Will and Gareth and Darius, there are tens of thousands of kids running around imagining that they can leap straight from their job as a waitress, or a position teaching children, to solo stardom. They can't. Why? Because Lionel Richie couldn't – he was in the Commodores before he enjoyed solo fame. And because Ricky Martin couldn't – he was in a boy-band called Menudo. And there are dozens of other examples. For example:

Bobby Brown was in New Edition
Phil Collins was in Genesis
Beyoncé Knowles was in Destiny's Child
Ronan Keating was in BoyZone
Diana Ross was in the Supremes
Annie Lennox was in the Eurythmics
Björk was in the Sugarcubes
George Michael was in Wham!
Robbie Williams was in Take That

In fact, you can count the number of pop superstars who emerged fully formed as a solo artist on one hand: Elvis, Madonna and precious few others. Throughout this book, I have used Justin Timberlake as an example of a present-day artist who correctly established himself long before his solo career even began. His main move, of course, was being in 'N Sync, although dating Britney Spears didn't hurt. If Justin Timberlake hadn't been in 'N Sync, no record company would have invested millions of its own money in him. He would have been an unknown with a nice enough personality, but without a great voice and without any known songwriting talent. For that matter, Michael Jackson, had he not been the lead singer of the Jackson Five, would never have become the most famous man on the planet. He first became a household name as the lead singer of a group, and without that group it's unlikely anyone would have taken a chance on him at 14, 16 or even 18. As immensely talented as he was, as ambitious as he was, he would have still been an unknown.

Another Jackson, Janet, followed a different course, but one that I also highly recommend.

She began her career on television, with small roles on shows like *Good Times* and *Diff'rent Strokes*, while she was still a little girl. This is an extremely wise move, because it's founded on a sound business principle – when you're starting off in an industry, you go where the work is, and there are many more opportunities for small parts on television than there are empty spots for artists at record labels. In Janet Jackson's case, it paid off a decade later, when she decided she wanted to be a pop singer. Since the road was already paved, both by her family name and her TV career, she had a smoother course on her way to stardom. The same thing goes for Alanis Morissette, who knew that she wanted to be a pop star when she was just a young girl. Rather than beat her head against the door for years, she worked on a Canadian kids' show, *You Can't Do That On Television*, for a few years, made a name for herself, and then became a pop performer. (I have to say that what Alanis achieved is close to a miracle. To me she is a more successful illusionist than David Copperfield.) Britney Spears and Christina Aguilera were in the *Mickey Mouse Club*. Kylie Minogue was signed because she was already a big star on the Australian soap opera, *Neighbours*. And that's how Natalie Imbruglia got signed as well. Jennifer Lopez was a dancer on *In Living Color*. For that matter, my own success with Robson and Jerome proves this rule beyond any shadow of a doubt. They were not singers. They were actors on a British television show. That's how they were known and how they wanted to be known. But when they had the opportunity to make pop records, the public had no problem accepting them in their new incarnation. My point is this: they were already entertainers. The public already knew who they were.

If you have the opportunity to get a part on a television show, no matter how small it seems, take it.

Use Your Connections

There are exceptions to these rules, of course, like Eminem, but that's just the result of utter genius sweetened by luck. His timing was immaculate, his songs are sensational, he has tabloid appeal and he cuts across all races. And even Eminem, if you look more closely, had more than just his talent to recommend him: he came onto the scene closely associated with Dr Dre, who was already an established producer. From the start, Eminem used his professional connections as well as his rivalries to elevate himself. A more recent example is 50 Cent, who was endorsed by both Eminem and Dr Dre and became a huge star in his own right. The other good example of stardom by association was Whitney Houston, who was already known to people in the record industry because her mother was Cissy Houston, a session singer, and her aunt is Dionne Warwick. This was an accident of birth, and if you're not Dionne Warwick's niece, there's nothing you can do about it, but my point is that you need something that will help make you familiar to the record label when you first appear.

I hope that what I'm communicating is that it's just as hard for the record labels as it is for the artists, but in a different way. They are operating under tremendous pressure to find and market the right stars, and they aren't willing to take risks. Since they'll be playing it safe, you have to put them at ease picking you. As somebody who gets paid a lot of money to find talent in pop music for an international label, I speak from experience – I am never just looking for a talent, but rather a talent with a head start. The business is too expensive now just to find somebody with a good voice and a good image, to mould them and refine them, and to then sit back and hope and pray that the public latches on. Trust me – the pop market is changing. When I look at any pool of people who are already in the entertainment industry, whether they're bit players on a TV show or a dance ensemble on a kids' show, I'm looking for future stars. If I spot one in that group, I know that I may be able to turn him or her into a star. In other words, history will help you. Put yourself in the frame of mind of the record label: they're thinking 'Make my job easy for me!' Finally, to prove my point, who is No. 1 on the American charts at the time of writing? Hilary Duff, TV actress turned singer.

Find Good Material

When I came back from America after my first long stretch away, I switched on some of the music channels and started watching them for a while to re-acclimatize myself to what was happening over here. I have to say I was depressed. Much of the problem is the crap material. One of the reasons Take That did so well was that Gary Barlow wrote some good songs, like *Pray* and, obviously, *Back For Good*, that were mixed up with some very carefully chosen covers. But if you're signing an artist who doesn't write their own material you have to be able to tap in to successful songwriting talent.

One of the best songwriters in the world for pop – in fact probably the best pop songwriter in the world now – is a guy called Jurge Elofson. He's about 45 years old, and he's one of the most talented and insecure people I've ever met. His ability to take situations and write songs to match them is unparalleled. It's a kind of genius. I remember saying to him in the middle of the first series of *Pop Idol* one day, 'I need a song that typifies what the person who wins this competition is going to feel at the moment after all the pain, after all the anguish, after all the hype. That person will be standing on the stage alone; what will he or she be feeling at that moment in time?'

Two weeks later he phoned me. 'Let me play you a chorus, Simon.' I waited and then it came on: 'I'm gonna take this moment, and make it last forever, I'm gonna take this night and make it evergreen.' I couldn't believe it. It was just so right. Jurgen has written a ton of the Westlife records, some of the Gareth Gates hits, songs for Kelly Clarkson and others. But in the main there is a lack of good songwriting teams, which is why so many of the pop records today sound bland.

The point is this: whether or not you're working with a record label, a pop star needs to have good songs. As a result, you need to find your way to the best songwriters and producers in the world. In simplistic terms, most good songwriters are whores. They go where the money is. And in any given year, you have somewhere between half a dozen and a dozen of what I would call grade-A pop songs. These are career records, and they're songs like 'Baby One More Time' (by Britney Spears), 'Beautiful' (Christina Aguilera), 'Hero' (Enrique Iglesias), 'Livin' La Vida Loca' (Ricky Martin), 'Torn' (Natalie Imbruglia), 'Can't Get You Out Of My

Head' (Kylie), 'No Matter What' (BoyZone) and so forth. Put yourself in the place of the people who are writing these kinds of songs. They don't come along very often. So why should you, as a writer, waste one of your grade-A songs on an unknown, when every artist and record label is lining up to record that material? If you give the song to the unknown, you may make him or her very happy, but you may not sell records. If you give the song to Christina Aguilera, you're guaranteed to sell three to six million albums worldwide. In the end, I tend to think it's the song that's more powerful than the performer, because I can think of at least a few cases where careers that were quite wounded were brought back to life by brilliant songs: Cher's 'Believe' is one example; Kylie Minogue's 'Can't Get You Out Of My Head' is another. It's a catch-22 situation: without the hit songs, artists don't have careers, but without careers, they're not going to have access to the hit songs. That's the brilliant stroke of *Pop Idol* – we are able to take these talented singers and pair them with material that even established artists would kill to record.

If that's the brilliance of *Pop Idol*, though, it's also the most obvious example of how the show creates an unreal world. To any singer who doesn't have access to a hit network television programme as his or her launching pad, I would recommend finding your way to the top producers and songwriters and attaching yourself to them in any way you can. You probably won't get their grade-A material, but if they like you and believe in your talent, you may get something – their grade-B material, or their grade-C material, or even their grade-D material. And anything from a top producer or songwriter is better than nothing; even if they just speak well of you in the industry, you'll be associated with their success. If, for example, as a new singer, you were able to get the Neptunes' writing and production team to agree to work with you, I guarantee at least six major record labels would offer you a contract. And I know for a fact that songwriters and production teams, while they're not exactly easy to get in contact with, are easier to reach than the heads of record labels. Again, new artists need to be smart about their careers and take the path of lesser resistance when first establishing their names.

Final Judgement

The Best Pop Singles of All Time

Whitney Houston, 'I Will Always Love You'
This song showed her off perfectly. If you were going to rank a song and a vocal performance, you'd rank this a 10. You can't fault it.

The Righteous Brothers, 'Unchained Melody'

This song has something really unique about it – it is almost impossible to get tired of it. The structure is part of the reason; it's not organized like a traditional song, which is why it's called 'Unchained Melody'. But it also has this amazing ability to sell emotion. If it's used in the right context, it's the saddest and most beautiful song in the world. I have had a number of artists record it, and every time it has sold over a million copies. If I found the right singer, I would do it again.

Sinead O Connor 'Nothing Compares To You'

A classic example of how one song can make the singer an overnight sensation. In my opinion, it is one of the best singles of all time.

Britney Spears, 'Baby One More Time'

If you ever had to define the perfect pop single, this is it. It's more than a hit single – it's a career song.

Elvis Presley, 'Suspicious Minds'

Perfection.

The Beatles, 'She Loves You'

This probably changed the sound of pop music forever.

Get Representation

To get good material – or, for that matter, to get a recording contract, you're going to need someone to fight for you and champion you: in other words, you're going to need good representation.

A singer with a credible agent looks more legitimate to the outside world, and he or she will obviously have an easier time getting in the door of a record label. Managers make things happen because they have track records, because they have the time to talk to many different labels, and because they have a history of success with record labels, and of course experience and expertise. And it is a talent, to be sure – I have dealt with many managers in my time, and it's hard to be tough on behalf of your client without alienating the companies that are footing the bill. Still, a good manager is an absolute necessity, because I have never, ever met anyone in my life who got a record deal by sending in an unsolicited tape. They don't get listened to – and if they do, the person who's doing the listening is a junior employee without any power to make a deal. In other words, it's a complete waste of time.

If a manager decides to take you on, it will only be because they think they can do some good for you, and you can do some good for them. Because of that, you should research your representation before seeking it out; certain managers specialize in certain kinds of acts. It's pointless going to somebody who looks after rock bands if you want to be a pop star. Using normal channels – the internet is probably your best bet – you should be able to do all the research you need in a few weeks, and that will help you get a tape to whoever you think might be a good manager. And remember, managers, while not exactly simple to get to, are easier to contact than some other people in the industry. Louis Walsh, who put together Westlife and BoyZone, is more likely to take your call or listen to your tape than the head of BMG Records or Sony Records.

With that said, you should remember that managers need to be courted just like anyone else. When you send your package, make sure that everything about your presentation is professional and inviting. Good photos are something we always look for when we receive a package. Another thing that is quite important, though it may sound strange, is how the package is sealed and addressed: if it's written all in scribbles and bound up with acres of masking tape, it's likely to end up in the dustbin. By the same token, if you're able to set up a meeting with a prospective manager, act professional. One piece of important advice: demonstrate that you know your business and that you can find a niche. (Is the biggest boy band in the world about to fall off in popularity?

Is the top female solo star about to take a tumble? If so, then it's time to replace them, and any potential manager should know that you understand this.) Don't do the obvious – Manager: 'Why are you here?' Singer: 'Because I want to be famous.' Follow the same rules, in short, that you would for an audition, because it is an audition. In a sense, it's the most important audition of your career.

Put In The Hard Work

Pop Idol comes at a strange time in the history of our pop culture. Today, kids are lazier than ever and think they're entitled to something. Often we have people who come in to see us in the auditions, people with good enough singing voices, and when we ask them if they have taken any lessons, they say no proudly. They shouldn't be proud. This isn't all about natural ability. In a way, being a pop singer is no different from being a great athlete. If you want to run the hundred metres in ten seconds, you aren't going to do it without a coach. Many people start with talent, but you've got to train to hone your talent. If you're a runner, that means learning how to get off the blocks more quickly than anybody else and practising until you perfect your form. Generally, I have very little patience for anybody who isn't prepared to put in 15-hour days at the start of their career.

While singing is hard work, it's not hard labour: the contestants had to rehearse, do interviews, go into studios, but generally they travelled in style, in luxury limousines. Sometimes we would ask contestants why they were on *Pop Idol*, and they would tell us that they had prepared their whole life for this chance. Hearing that always made me want to laugh. Their whole life? Give me a break. These kids were 17 years old. If you want a senior management position in a normal business, you can't expect to get it in five seconds. You've got to work your way up. In my case, I always knew I wanted to end up on top, but I never assumed that it would be my next stop after the postroom. There's a myth in this business that if you don't hit by the time you're 25, you'll never make it. That's total rubbish. If you look at some of the biggest artists in the world, some of them are older – Sheryl Crow, for example, or Tina Turner, or Cher. The biggest touring band in the world is still the Rolling Stones and they're not exactly spring chickens. No one is governed by age. Some of them kick around in the business for a while before they get their break.

I think, strangely enough, that *Pop Idol* and then *American Idol* have magnified the entitlement problem. It shows these young singers enjoying what is, essentially, impossible success, and so many viewers start to feel as though they, too, will be plucked from obscurity. That's just as crazy as thinking that you're going to win the lottery. Even on the show I have seen this problem. In either season, it was clear from the first or second week who the finalists would be. There were some performers who, try as they might, were never going to make it into the top three. Part of my job, I always felt, was to tell them that. If I let Korben entertain for one moment the thought that he might win, I would have been fuelling his delusion. If I let Hayley go on thinking she was going to be the next Pop Idol, I would have been lying to her. Sometimes I just want to prick the bubble of what I regard as this self-absorbed egotism. This isn't to say that those two contestants – or any other contestant – can't make it eventually, only that they have lots of work ahead of them. When singers get voted off, many of them feel that their apprenticeship in the entertainment industry has ended, and they wind up at home, sitting by the phone, waiting for a call from a record executive. That's ridiculous. The truth, of course, is that their apprenticeships have just begun. They have a head start because they have been on national television, and they should use that to their advantage, but their careers are still in their infancy.

The Best Pop Stars

Robbie Williams Recently, I did an interview with a newspaper and I said that I didn't like Robbie's new single, which I didn't. But the truth is that I like Robbie as a bloke and, more importantly, I think he's the best pop star England has, bar none. What he has, compared to so many of these people, is the X Factor: that individuality, personality, unpredictability. If you put Ronan Keating on *CD UK* now I could tell you exactly what he's going to say: 'God bless you, thank you very much, love everybody.' No one learns anything. No one feels anything. I think it can get boring. If you put Robbie Williams on *CD UK*, I haven't got a bloody clue what he's going to say or how he will behave. That's why I would tune in, and that's why I love him.

Kylie Minogue I love Kylie Minogue because I love anyone who can reinvent themselves. I loved Kylie in the beginning. I thought she was sensational. Then she went through this embarrassing middle stage, with her alternative rock records. It just didn't work and was difficult to watch, because it was just like trying to put a square in a circle. When I heard 'Spinning Around', however, I loved it, and then I found it was Kylie Minogue. She was very clever in that video because she realised that her voice was not the most important part of her career but rather her bum, and she exploited that to the full. I mean in that video it was 90 per cent shot on her arse. Then the second album came out and I heard 'Can't Get You Out Of My Head', and to this day it is one of the best pop records of all time. The video was superb, the song was amazing, she was amazing in it, and it just proves the point. You can reinvent yourself, actually not through image but through great pop songs.

Elton John If you'd have asked me if I liked Elton John a year ago, I'd have said, 'No.' Then I met him, and I have to admit I was impressed, because when you meet Elton John you are meeting a star with a capital S. I went to his party in Windsor with Louis, Westlife's manager, and, to be honest, I was suspicious. Elton had been slagging me off in the press, saying all I was interested in was money and that *Pop Idol* was a disgrace etc, etc. I thought, 'He's obviously invited me down to humiliate me or something.'

But Louis said, 'No, he'd really like to meet you.'

So I turned up at the party and it was, without question, one of the best parties I've ever been to. I've never seen anything like it in my life. An amazing evening: celebrity after celebrity after celebrity, the venue was just mind-blowing, the food was sensational, and the entertainment was incredible. Elton sang, Barry Manilow sang, Donna Summer sang. At one point, Elton rushed up to my table saying, 'Isn't she fantastic?' It was good to see he is also still a fan. He was good fun, a great host, and what pop music actually is all about. He has incredible talent, and his songs will last forever, but he's also excessive and a star. To me, that's pop music.

Busted There was only one artist who I tried to sign in the past two years, and unfortunately I didn't get the deal, and that was Busted. I forget who tipped me off about this band, but somebody said there's a band looking for a deal at the moment and you should get hold of the demo. I was blown away. I thought their songs were very good, I just heard hit after hit after hit. Then I found out that they co-wrote their own material and played instruments. Amazing. I asked for a meeting, and the band came in, the three boys and the manager. I didn't like the manager at all, but I loved the boys. We played the demos again, and I was impressed. 'I think I can turn you into, without question, in 12 months the biggest pop band in the UK,' I said. Then I asked where their drummer was. They shrugged. 'That's crazy,' I said. 'You're playing your own instruments. It looks ridiculous and sounds ridiculous.' Maybe I shouldn't have insisted on this, but I was right. Over the next few weeks, I tried every-thing. I offered them a huge deal, promised the moon. In the end, I think that the manager might have worried that I would undermine his authority, and they signed elsewhere. Now obviously they've gone on to be very, very successful, but I actually do believe that if they'd signed to my label I would have made them even bigger stars. They are the best pop band since Westlife. They can potentially have massive success all over the world, and this Christmas, I predict, they will be the No. 1 pop band in the country.

Dido I love Dido because she's just talented through and through. She's very lucky because she has an amazing collaborator in her brother Rolo, who is one of the best writer/producers in the UK at the moment. Put the two of them together and it really is the perfect collaboration. I've met her in real life and she's fabulous, just a really, really nice person, level-headed and grounded.

Daniel Bedingfield I think Daniel is odd. But genius is strange and I think this guy is a genius. I think he is potentially the best singer/songwriter since Elton John and he is going to be around for a very long time.

The Worst Pop Stars

Ms Dynamite I think she's the most over-hyped artist in the last 10 years. She shot to fame for winning the Mercury Music Award, and I remember hearing one of her records for the first time and worrying that I might be out of touch. It just sounded like crap to me. She looks the part, she wears the right clothes, she's got the right accent. Do I rate her as a worldwide artist? No. Would I want her on my record label? No. I think it's hype over substance, I just don't get it. I couldn't hum five seconds of a Miss Dynamite record. She has also caused problems for me on the show; a lot of artists we see now at *Pop Idol* are trying to copy Ms Dynamite's songs. The problem is, to me, they're not good songs. She's cool to like and I'm the only A&R guy in England who will say this.

Craig David I think Craig David might have lost the plot professionally. I remember hearing his records at the beginning, and thinking that he was pleasant enough, but nothing special, like a male Sade. If you listen to a song like 'Seven Days' it's not that much different from what Sade was doing years ago. But then I began to hear him in interviews talking about himself in the third person saying things like, 'I think Craig David's going to be huge in America', you start to see a problem. Then there was a huge uproar when he didn't win a Brit Award and he then went on stage and rapped about the injustice in the third person. When you meet him he's a nice guy. I like him. Craig's problem is he was launched in the same way as Lisa Stansfield and Seal. Record producers had him front the first single. The single was massive, a star is born. I personally hated the second album, the songs were weak and you begin to wonder if it could all be over.

Mark Owen He wasn't the best singer in Take That, but he was the cute little one who all the girls adored. It's great to have someone like that in a band. When Take That broke up, he was signed to BMG as a solo artist, which seemed like the right move. He could have been an English David Cassidy. We were all invited down to his showcase at Abbey Road, and the whole scene was like something out of *This is Spinal Tap*. It was just the most ludicrous evening I've ever spent in my life. The police were informed in St John's Wood that at least 10,000 girls would be outside Abbey Road Studios, so they practically closed off the road and brought in all these extra policemen and security guards. I turned up and there were at most 20 girls, more policemen than fans. Then we went into the recording studio, and in walked Mark Owen with this band. He looked like he hadn't showered for a week, his hair was a mess, and his songs were even worse. Incredibly, they were a horrid stab at alternative rock. At one point he did a cover version of Radiohead's *Creep*, and in the middle threw himself on the floor in a sort of state of artistic mental anguish. He looked like an insect, writhing with his arms and legs in the air, screaming obscenities into the microphone and yet six months before he was singing 'Babe' dressed in a soldiers outfit. Normally when an artist finishes their set there's a pretence that there won't be an encore, the band shout 'Good night' – which means 'I'll be back in five minutes.' When Mark ran backstage, there was a stampede to get out of the studio. It was career suicide, and it was followed by one of those awful *Big Brother* shows, which resurrected his career enough to get him a record deal. Nice guy, bad instincts.

Dear Simon Cowell,

I have a message for you. As you think you are so clever perhaps you would try and fill in the missing letters to find out what all my family really thinks about you.

Y _ U A _ E A C_MP L_TE W_NK_R

Have fun
Regards

Mr Drake

Once you decide to devote yourself to a pop career, you're going to spend much of your time in audition rooms. As *Pop Idol* and *American Idol* prove, audition rooms are where entertainment careers are born – or where they die a premature death. It's vital to know how to handle the audition process. And while I have spent the last two years watching people walk through the *American Idol* rooms, I have spent the last 25 years in the business. It's very difficult to advise on this because if you are good, you're good, and if you're crap, you're crap. Anyway, here are my top ten tips for auditions.

1. Don't copy another performer. I'd say that 90 per cent of the people who come to our auditions, no matter how talented they are, have perfected only the art of mimicry.

They have listened to an artist they like countless times – Mariah Carey is probably the most common model at the moment – and they are certain that they can succeed by copying a success. But what we're looking for is somebody original. The biggest stars you can think of, and the most enduring, may be similar to other stars, but they are still unquestionably unique. There is only one Elton John. There is only one Madonna. There is only one Cher. There was only one Frank Sinatra. And there is only one Michael Jackson, thank God.

2. Don't overstyle yourself. You see this all the time. My interpretation of somebody who overdresses for an audition is that they're desperate. What we're looking for is people who are comfortable in their own skin, and when we see people come in with hats, things around their wrists, one trouser leg tucked carefully into a boot, it just looks like an act. I don't believe in underdressing – I think you've got to look as if you're serious – but this overdetermined-pop-star look is absolutely loathsome. Sunglasses are a complete no-no.

3. Don't sing and dance at the same time. First of all, it smacks of cabaret. And also, it's very difficult to dance when you're singing without a backing track. You'll

likely run out of breath. I always advise against singing and dancing. Some of the worst auditions we've seen on *Pop Idol* are the singer/dancers. Remember 'YMCA'?

4. Make eye contact when performing. This is a sign of confidence. When you're doing an audition and you're gazing up to the ceiling, it's very difficult for us to know what's going on in your head. You seem nervous and unsure of yourself. It's a simple, small thing, but very important.

5. Choose the right song for your personality. I can't stress this enough: there are songs that are right for your voice and your personality, and songs that are wrong. One of the most off-putting things we see when we're on the road is a 16-year-old girl who walks in, looks very hip, and then sings a Patsy Cline song. To me that doesn't make sense.

6. Don't grovel when you come in. Again, I look upon it as an act of desperation. So many times people come in and they come up with this terrible dialogue about how much they like me or Pete or Nicki. It's demeaning, and there's no point to it. We're not looking to find a nice person; we're looking for somebody who's confident and assured, but talented above all. Trust me, most stars aren't nice.

7. Believe in yourself the second you leave the house. Self-possession isn't something you can turn on seconds before you walk into the audition room. People like Will or Gareth believed in themselves from the minute they woke up in the morning. If you try to cobble it together in the waiting room, you'll fail.

8. Be sure to eat and drink prior to an audition. Food is fuel, and you don't want to run out of fuel. Over and over again, I have seen people forget the words, or start to get emotional. When I ask them when they last ate, and they say, 'Twenty-four hours ago', I lose my patience. This sounds like silly advice, but it's important.

9. Rehearse. When Michael Jackson was asked the three most important things for aspiring stars, he said, 'Rehearse, rehearse, rehearse.' You need to know your material well enough that it's second nature. If you have to try to remember the lyrics, you'll lose your confidence.

10. Listen. Sometimes a judge or a talent executive will see something in you but want you to try something slightly different. Sometimes they'll want you to try something entirely different. When I say to a contestant, 'You're not picking the right material for your voice', or 'You need to

take singing lessons', or 'Your hair looks awful', I'm not
saying it because I like to be critical – or rather, I'm not
saying it only because I like to be critical. I'm saying it
because it's true. Be receptive to suggestions, and recognize that someone with experience in the music business
might be able to see something in you that you don't see
in yourself. In other words, stop sulking.

Embracing Celebrity

Let's say that you're lucky enough to get to the second stage
in your career, that as a result of your perseverance, your
connections and/or your wonderful auditions, you have
joined a band or landed a small role on a television show.
Now you need to take it one stage further. So what do you
do? Easy: date a celebrity.

Elizabeth Hurley is now one of the most famous people
on the planet. How did she get famous? She dated Hugh
Grant. Of course, while she was dating Hugh Grant, she
turned up for a premiere in a Versace dress that was literally
held together with safety pins. But the fact that she was
with Hugh Grant, the fact that she was his girlfriend, got
her photographed in every newspaper in the world. For a
while there, she was the name in bold next to his, the name
that readers didn't quite know but that they knew they

should know. That was an incredibly effective way of launching a career.

Pardon me for being cynical, but I believe that quite a few celebrity couples are at least partly the result of PR illusions. Quite often relationships between stars are genuine, but just as often they are skilful ways of getting a relative unknown into the spotlight. When you're an aspiring celebrity and you pair off with another aspiring celebrity, you don't just double or triple your exposure. Rather, you multiply it by a factor of ten or 20. People in the media are fascinated, and always have been, by the idea that famous or even semi-famous people are shagging each other. Look at how many stars change mates just before the opening of a new film, or before the release of a new album. P. Diddy said something a little while ago that got him ridiculed in the press – he said that he pioneered the trend of celebrities dating celebrities. But in a way he's right. When he had his relationship with J. Lo, both of their careers went through the roof afterwards. J. Lo learned this lesson well – her relationship with Ben Affleck, while it may well have had something to it, was also a canny PR move, *Gigli* notwithstanding. The same thing goes for Beyoncé and Jay-Z; it's one of the least likely pairings on earth, but tabloids love to write about it and speculate. And then, of course, Demi Moore and Ashton Kutcher: add one not-very-respected young actor and one not-so-remembered ageing actress, and what do you have? The top entertainment story of the year.

You may think I'm joking, but I'm completely serious. Entertainment careers are all about momentum and coverage, and relationships are an important part of that. And remember, celebrity relationships don't even have to be normal. If Ricky Martin ever bothered to give me a call and ask my advice, I'd tell him to snap up a celebrity girlfriend, and quick.

Simon as Cupid
Predictions for Today's Top Celebrity Couples

Brad Pitt and Jennifer Aniston: True love

Ashton Kutcher and Demi Moore: Won't last a year

Jay-Z and Beyoncé: Dubious

Ben Affleck and J. Lo: Won't last a year*

David Beckham and Victoria Beckham: True love

Justin Timberlake and Cameron Diaz: Dubious

Guy Ritchie and Madonna: True love

Paul McCartney and Heather Mills: True love

Michael Jackson and anyone: Dubious

P. Diddy and himself: True love

*In the two days since I compiled this list, Affleck and J. Lo have broken off their engagement.

Staying on Top

Once you have made it to the top – wherever your particular top may be – maintaining your fame is extremely tricky. Many stars fall from their perch so rapidly that they lose their dignity along with their reputation. Take Prince, for example. For a time, he was arguably one of the most famous people on the planet. He could do no wrong. He was selling tens of millions of records a year, filling stadiums, making movies, and then at some point it just stopped. As an outsider, it seemed to me that he had ceased to reside in reality, that he had lost touch with all aspects of his artistry and career. That general piece of advice – don't lose touch – is getting harder and harder as the pop-culture climate distorts fame and breeds a certain sense of entitlement. Here are some other important points to remember:

Don't make any sudden moves. Stars like Elvis Presley and Frank Sinatra understood – or their management understood – what got them to the top. Most notably, they understood the value of working with great songwriters, and there was a trust between artist and management that endured. But many pop stars let their fame go to their head, and at some point they decide that they want to write their own songs. The rationales are insane: they want to 'move on', or 'change their audience'. Well, it's risky, certainly, in pop music. Kylie Minogue, after five years in the wilderness, after putting out two disastrous indie rock albums that she felt better expressed her personality as an artist, came back to pop music with one of the strongest records of all time, 'Can't Get You Out Of My Head', and revived her international stardom. She didn't change her audience. She changed back to her original audience.

Don't start believing in your own genius. One of the best examples of career meltdown was an artist called Terence Trent D'Arby. An American-born British singer, he surfaced in the late eighties with one of the best debuts I have ever heard. It was sensational. He had a fantastic soul voice, lots of style, and he even wrote his own material. It didn't seem like there was any chance that he would fail. Around that time, I bumped into him, and to say I thought his head was up his own arse would have been the understatement of the year. Personally I found him arrogant, disconnected, and he seemed unfocused on everything but his own ego. People always say that success has changed this artist, or that one, but I find that success rarely changes anyone. Rather, it gives them the power to be what they always were. Terence Trent D'Arby went on like this, suddenly unconstrained by propriety, and when his second album came out, it was an all-time turkey. I have spoken with people who worked with him on that record, and evidently he had lost all sense of reality. He considered himself to be a god, some kind of infallible creative genius, and he wouldn't listen to any criticism. Well, he should have, because that second record killed his career. Recently, I saw that he has resurfaced with a new name – he's Sananda something-or-other – and a new record. He may creep back into people's consciousness, but he's nothing compared to what he could have been. Pop stars also have this funny career disease in which they begin to believe that they can write or co-write their songs. It's almost an unwritten rule that by the second or third album there are co-writing credits. It is my belief that writing a hit song is one of the hardest jobs on earth. And yet everyone believes they can do it. To my mind, this is ridiculous. Can you imagine creating a new TV show, hiring actors and then after a breakout year having the actors insist on writing the scripts and directing? It happens in some cases eventually, but nowhere near as quickly. Television stars accept that they're being highly paid for following someone else's direction and script. Pop stars have a problem with it. From a label's perspective, if you can find an artist who is a gifted songwriter – hallelujah! Those people are so rare that they're like the Loch Ness monster. If one appears, get a photograph to prove that he or she exists.

Don't think you can go it alone. Artists also let their egos destroy their relationships with their mentors, and that's a fatal error. Many artists are young. They are talented but inexperienced, and they desperately need people to tell them which way is up. One of the best mentors in this business is Clive Davis, who was the head of Arista Records and now runs RCA/J Records in America. He is in his early seventies, and as a result he knows about a thousand times more than an 18-year-old kid. It's true that pop music is a youth market, but it's also a business. Clive usually attaches himself to artists early on, and those artists tend to remain viable for many years. He was a mentor for Whitney Houston, for Carlos Santana, for so many others. If they have listened to him, they have increased their chances of survival. Similarly, my friend Simon Fuller managed the Spice Girls. After two successful albums they fired him because they thought they knew better. Goodbye, Spice Girls.

Don't pay too little attention to what people say about you. I have always explained to the Idols that they were all in a unique position in the entertainment industry, because they were effectively the people's champions. The general public were asked to give their opinion on who was the most entertaining, or the most talented, or the most compelling, and they voted for you. They created you. And, quite literally, without them you're nothing. If you drift too far away from that anchor, if you forget about the people who put you on the top, you'll become unglued. So any day, at any time, if anyone asks for your autograph or wants to shake your hand, don't turn away. Instead, remember how much you relied on these people. The Idols came into this business to become famous. The public made their dream come true.

Don't stop working. The artists who endure are the ones who stay focused even after they have reached the top of their profession. I saw it with Madonna. I see it with Beyoncé. I see it with J. Lo. I used to see it with Michael Jackson. Remember, in this business there's always someone younger and hungrier coming up behind you.

Even if an artist behaves impeccably, staying famous is by no means guaranteed. Today's market, especially for pop singles, is ailing. What I used to love about pop music was the fact that there were only one or two record companies making unashamed pop records. We were always kind of the minority. But at the moment, it seems that everyone else has decided to get on the bandwagon. I think it's economics; they must feel that pop music is an easy buck and a good way to save their jobs. As a result, you have people who only a few years ago were making rock and alternative records suddenly signing pop acts. But that just saturates the market, which can only sustain a relatively small number of good pop artists.

The saturation has hurt many aspects of the record business, not the least of which is the pleasure of topping the charts. Two years ago, or even a year ago, being No. 1 in the charts really meant something. Songs would get to the top and stay there; Bryan Adams and Wet Wet Wet stuck it out for months. But as records sell fewer and fewer copies, it's less and less important. Now, it's not uncommon to have a new No. 1 every week.

The turnover is also the result of frontloading sales. In the old days, a record might enter at 80, and then steadily climb over a number of weeks: 70 to 50 to 18 to 12 to 3 to 2 to 1. These days, labels have perfected ways of alerting the consumer to a record's release, and in general everyone buys records on the first day of release. There's no drama any more; the pop charts have lost the sense of plot that made them so exciting to watch.

We also have to rethink the artists we make famous. One of the things that made Oasis so successful was their behaviour: bad behaviour, admittedly, but interesting behaviour. If you turned a lens on them for any length of time, you were going to get something newsworthy. Now, we've got to the point where our artists are so perfectly handled and manicured that they don't have anything to say any longer, except careerist babble. When I hear artists on *CD UK* talking about chart positions, record sales, territories they'd like to crack, I think, 'You're 18 years old, you should be talking about going out, getting laid and having a great time.' I don't see any personalities any more. We had a touch of that on *Pop Idol*, in fact, when Gareth got in the papers over his affair with Jordan. We had some concern, certainly, but I remember thinking that if I was 17 years old and a very successful glamour model knocked on my bedroom door, I'd have definitely invited her in.

Since we have spoken about the artists who have bombed spectacularly after huge success, we should also look at some artists who've had enduring popularity. Barbra Streisand can be out of the news for five years, but if she announced tomorrow that she was holding a concert, it would probably sell out faster than any concert on earth. She is like one of those movie stars from the forties – she lives in the mansion on the hill, the public knows a little bit about her private life, but she's not plastered all over the tabloids every day. In fact, she's almost the opposite of Madonna – while Madonna gives it all away in each incarnation and then has to remake herself to replenish her mystique, Barbra Streisand keeps her distance, is a little cooler, but is no less respected. Of the newer crop, I think that Justin Timberlake really is a force to be reckoned with. Whether he was advised to plan his career the way he did, or whether he instinctively knew how, he understood the point of springboard appeal. From 'N Sync, and being Britney Spears's boyfriend, he has evolved into a fully-fledged star. Beyoncé has also done everything right up to this point: she began in Destiny's Child, has done some acting to establish herself as more than a singer, and has a high-profile relationship with another entertainer. She seems entirely determined to stay on top and, in time, become one of the great pop stars. And Jennifer Lopez has that same ultimate determination that has defined many of pop's biggest names. She will go to any length to stay in the public eye, and her quality control is incredible. Those are the people who I really believe are special. They are definitely not the best singers around. But look into their eyes and you will see real determination and hunger. What links all of these artists? Ambition with a capital 'A'.

The *Idol* shows have run for two years, winning huge audiences and launching the careers of some of the most exciting young singers in the world. I was there at the beginning, and I was there in the middle and I may well be there at the end, whenever that is. If I had to distil one lesson from this entire process – and from the two decades I spent in the record business before *American Idol* was a gleam in anyone's eye – it would be that entertainers do not rise to the top of their craft, or even to the middle, without determination. Determination is an overused word, and the idea has become something of a cliché, but it's vital and it's true. In my career I've had 34 No. 1 singles. I've sold over 90 million records. I have broken all sorts of world records for artists having the most consecutive No. 1 singles, but when I was starting off it didn't come easily to me. When I eventually got the job I wanted, I was told many, many times that what I was doing wasn't good enough. I was never happy about it, but there was something in the back of my mind that told me that my critics were right, and not particularly malicious, and I resolved to get better so that I could create the proper opportunities for myself. And I did.

There must be hundreds if not thousands of people today singing in hotel bars and local bands who are great singers. Talented, attractive, charismatic – the whole package. But they don't have the determination to take it further. They have reached their comfort zone. If Madonna wasn't Madonna and you found her in the Holiday Inn in Detroit singing 'Evergreen', you would not necessarily think of her as a woman who could be the biggest recording artist in the world. It was her determination and confidence that turned her into a pop star, her idea of herself as superior that separated her from the rest of the pack. When people get turned down by us on *Pop Idol*, some of them look deflated, like it's the end of the world. I would like to see some of them resurface a year later, or three years later, with a new image, a better sense of their talent and a career. It would be inspiring to me if some of the *Pop Idol* losers became stars of the same magnitude as the winners. It would speak of their focus and ambition. It would prove many different wonderful things about the record industry, all at once.

To be a recording artist selling records around the world is probably the best job anyone could ever hope to have. The business is unpredictable and ruthless, but the rewards are potentially huge. And what makes it all so wonderful is – it could be you.

(If you can sing.)

Dear Mr Cowell,

Can you sing? Probably not. Do you know what it is like to go onstage? No you don't.

I would like to offer my opinion of you since you do it to people on PopIdol.

You are arrogant, rude, your hair is a mess, you talk with a plum in your mouth and your trousers come up to your neck. I bet you don't like that do you?

The trouble with people like you is you stop people like me getting a break. I have been singing in clubs for over 20 years and I can tell you this. Robbie Williams isn't fit to be my backing singer. None of you know anything anymore. Where are the Val Doonicans or the Harry Secombes of this world? I'll tell you, they have been run out of the business by people like you.

I hope someone you hate wins the show.

Mr J

The second series of *Pop Idol* in 2003 was fun to be involved with and once again proved hugely popular with the viewing public. The final show in December attracted 11 million viewers, with more than 10 million people voting on the night. I'd had my doubts about a second series at the end of the previous one, and I walked away at the end of the evening knowing for sure this was the last *Pop Idol* show I would appear on.

The competition had had its fair share of controversy. For different reasons both Michelle McManus and Marc Dillon gave the press a field day, but when a story about Susanne Manning appeared in the tabloids I was furious. The story suggested that Susanne was a troublemaker and had got too big for her boots. It further claimed that she hated

Michelle McManus and had allegedly called her a 'fat cow'. I had no idea where the story came. Pete Waterman was equally as angry and said that Susanne was being bullied by the press. He even brought the subject up on one of the live shows, saying that he thought the stories were rubbish and it was unfair to Susanne because she had no platform from which to put the record straight. Unfortunately, once such stories are printed the public begins to believe them and the damage is done. It was a shame: I don't think Susanne ever recovered from that.

After the heats had finished – and before the first live show on 8 November – I thought Michelle had the best chance of winning, even though I still felt Roxanne was good enough to reach the finals. Susanne Manning was also a favourite because she had done so well in the wildcard show. Just before the live shows began I received a lot of calls from songwriters and the media asking me who I thought would win. I told them that if I had to choose now it would be Susanne. She still had that vulnerable quality, the public clearly liked her and her performance in the wildcard show had indeed been sensational. At that point I thought it would be an all-girl final between Michelle McManus and Susanne Manning – and most of the people I spoke to agreed that Susanne had the edge.

8 November – Elton John Night

I had got to know Elton quite well and had been to his amazing party in Windsor at which he had confessed to being a huge fan of *Pop Idol*. I never thought in a million years that we would be able to get him involved in the show...

The producers had arranged it so that Elton would turn up during rehearsals and surprise the contestants. He surprised them all right. The funniest moment of all was when Chris Hide saw Elton walk on – his jaw just dropped. It was fantastic television. It proved to be an interesting week altogether. Firstly, it was the one in which Mark Rhodes shone. He chose to sing 'Something About The Way You Look Tonight' and it just showed the importance of choosing the right song. Before this performance Mark had been on the verge of being eliminated but on the back of this one song he finished second overall that night. It was fantastic. Chris also did himself a lot of favours by choosing 'Circle Of Life'. All the finalists chose good songs apart from Kim Gee. Of all the Elton John songs to choose – and, let's face it, you are spoilt for choice – she managed to pick one called 'The One': frankly, I hadn't even heard of it. It was obvious right from the start that she was going to be voted off. Andy also did well with 'Can You Feel The Love Tonight?', which was another inspired choice. Michelle scraped through with her version of 'Your Song'. I'm afraid Roxanne could not do justice to 'Sorry Seems To Be The Hardest Word' – the song was just too big for her.

Overall, though, I thought Andy came out on top that night. The problem I had with Andy was that, although he now had greater confidence in himself, he was not ruthless enough to make it to the very top. He was just a nice guy with an OK voice. Kim went out that night and, when I spoke to her after the show, she didn't seem that bothered. Well, neither did we. She had done well to get as far as she had. Susanne got the majority of the votes that week with a massive 22.5%. I could no longer safely predict who was going to win this competition.

15 November – Disco Night

You'll know what I think about disco – 'the only time for great dance music' – but this show was a disco disaster. It was absolutely horrible and just didn't seem to work at all. In the first *Pop Idol* we had done Abba and that had been a disaster, too. There were some strange performances that night, the most bizarre being Chris Hide singing 'Ain't Nobody' by Chaka Kahn. Funnily enough, the audience loved him but I thought he was absolutely dreadful. Michelle sang 'If I Can't

Have You', which went down really well and was the best choice of song that night. Andy chose 'Rock With You' – but he just couldn't carry it off. I remember giving him a hard time that evening because he had shown zero emotion. Sam chose 'Blame It On The Boogie', the song Will Young performed when he auditioned on the first *Pop Idol*. I remember telling Sam that the minute he chose the right song for his voice he would have a real chance of winning the competition.

Susanne sang Candy Staton's 'Young Hearts Run Free', which wasn't good. She had started to look nervous and this was a weak performance. For the first time I could see her really struggling and I was concerned that this was all too much for her.

Andy was eliminated that week. His girlfriend, Michelle from Liberty X, was not happy. I was asked straight after the show if I would offer Andy a recording contract; I said no, because I didn't think we should be offering so many contracts when the show was all about having *one* winner. Michelle had shouted from the audience, 'What about Gareth Gates?' I replied that I thought Gareth was an exception. The first series of *Pop Idol* had been all about two people who had split the country. This year was very different and it was clear very early on that we would not be faced with the same situation again.

22 November – Beatles Night

The next live show was the Beatles show and we were all looking forward to it because we had never done it before. At this stage in the competition the frontrunners seemed to be Michelle, Chris, Susanne and Roxanne. If Roxanne was now looking like the perfect pop star, this proved to be the week that Sam came up trumps by choosing 'With A Little Help From My Friends': he did the soulful Joe Cocker version and he was amazing. It was the moment he really put his stamp on the competition and I thought he was the best by far, even though Michelle got the biggest percentage of votes on the night. Mark sang 'Help', which was pretty terrible; Roxanne chose 'Let It Be', which I thought would keep her in; Susanne sang a quirky version of 'Ticket To Ride' and it didn't work for her at all; Chris sang 'The Long And Winding Road', which was plain dreary.

To my utter horror, Roxanne was eliminated. Up to that point I had been absolutely convinced that Mark would be the one to go. I just couldn't believe the results. Mark got 13.7% of the vote and Roxanne 13.2%: it was that close. Roxanne was absolutely gutted – it's safe to say we all were. When I spoke to her after the show the poor girl was in pieces. What was clear now was that the public was taking into account other reasons to vote for its favourites.

The 'pop star' had been eliminated and I was starting to get puzzled.

After the Beatles show I remember telling Pete Waterman that I felt I no longer had much to offer any more. I had never said that before. I felt that I wasn't really doing my job. I liked Michelle McManus a lot and she would have been the one I would have voted for. I felt she needed my help. She was getting a lot of stick in the press about her weight and I couldn't help getting emotionally involved. What's more, we, the judges, were becoming caricatures of ourselves. It was all too contrived. We were expected to be controversial or critical. In the first series I had felt a real connection between the show and the way I did my job, but suddenly I no longer felt comfortable. I had also begun to wonder if, this year, we had really found ourselves a world-wide, international star. I felt that the winner might be based on personality and appeal rather than sheer talent. I was still enjoying the show but it had now become a peculiar experience for me.

29 November – Big Band Night

The Big Band Night is the one most contestants look forward to – and this show proved to be one of the best evenings we had in the second *Pop Idol* competition. There was one clear winner that night – Sam.

If the Big Band show had been the final, with five final-ists, Sam would have won it hands down. That night he got 34.2% of the vote, singing 'Mr Bojangles'. It was an extraordinarily versatile performance because he changed styles so many times during the song. To watch this little guy with bandy legs stand up and sing this song was just staggering. For me it was the highlight performance of the entire competition. Michelle sang Nina Simone's 'Feeling Good', and she sang it well, but for me the night belonged to Sam.

Mark chose a song I didn't know called 'Have You Met Miss Jones?' (it was covered by Robbie Williams on the soundtrack of *Bridget Jones's Diary*) – which I thought was a strange choice. Chris sang 'Ain't That A Kick In The Head' and really made the effort. I remember describing him as a cross between Dean Martin and Eric Morecambe. As I have said earlier, Chris wasn't one of my favourites and I had been rather scathing about him throughout the competition, but he started to grow on me at this point. I suddenly under-stood the appeal of this guy. He was so odd but he gave the show character because he was exactly the opposite of what you imagine a pop idol to be. And yet he was doing so well. I now wanted him to stay in.

Susanne sang 'Cry Me A River' and she just lost it on the night. I got the feeling that she knew she was going out.

When she was eliminated I thought to myself that she had had a pretty raw deal from the show. She had endured a negative press campaign which she did not deserve and her nerves had begun to get the better of her. It was a great pity and I felt very angry about those newspaper stories.

It was all beginning to look clear to me: Sam was now the front-runner. Everyone I spoke to in the street seemed to be behind him – particularly after the performance on the Beatles show. Pete Waterman was also rooting for him. I had a feeling that anything could happen in this series.

6 December – The Christmas Show

We had never done a Christmas show before and this one reminded me of an old-fashioned TV Christmas special I might have watched in the 1960s. I was relieved it all went well on the night because I had suggested the idea in the first place. It was a real feel-good experience. The only down side was the fact that Chris left that week.

Chris was eliminated principally because of his insipid version of the classic 'White Christmas', though I thought his 'Winter Wonderland' was a fantastic performance and certainly good enough to keep him in. I then predicted that Mark would be the one to go. Wrong again. Michelle was sensational that night. Her version of 'Oh Holy Night' was probably her best performance in the competition. It was the song I chose for her on the album and she was just brilliant.

Sam was also extremely good and he sang Wizzard's 'I Wish It Could Be Christmas Every Day'. He was gaining confidence and you felt there was real momentum behind him now. When it was announced that Chris had been eliminated I looked at Mark and thought, 'You jammy git!' Chris should not have gone that night. Now it was crystal-clear – we were heading for a Sam/Michelle final.

The Christmas Show was a very emotional night because that week I visited the house in which the contestants were living for the first time. I had to play them all the material they would be singing if they reached the final.

When I played Chris 'All This Time' he burst into tears. To be fair to Mark, I thought he was a great kid. It was a strange experience because while I was talking to them I could feel my whole attention focusing on Michelle and Sam, so convinced was I that they would be the two finalists. Mentally I think Sam was also certain that he would reach the final. In his own mind he was already there. Mark, on the other hand, appeared quietly resigned to the fact that he was going to be voted out. When the announcement came that Chris was out, Mark could hardly believe it. Neither could I.

13 December – Judges' Choice

This was the show in which the judges chose the songs. Two weeks before the show we had sat down with the producers to select two songs for each of the contestants. Quite a challenge given that we had been criticizing them throughout the competition for *their* choice of songs. At this stage Sam, Chris, Mark and Michelle were still in the competition.

We started with Sam, and someone – I can't remember who – suggested 'Maggie May'. Someone else suggested Bon Jovi's 'Always' – and this was the song that got Sam kicked out of *Pop Idol 2*.

Michelle was a little easier – big ballads. 'Without You' and 'Say A Little Prayer'. Of course at that time we had to choose songs for Mark not really believing he would be in the final three. We all assumed it would be Sam, Chris and Michelle. 'Back For Good' was a unanimous choice – but the killer song for him was 'If You Don't Know Me By Now', in my opinion one of the best pop songs of all time.

On the night of the show nothing had convinced us that it would be anything other than a Sam and Michelle final. When Mark came out and sang 'If You Don't Know Me By Now' I knew it was the best performance of the entire evening. Michelle did well, particularly with 'Say A Little Prayer', but overall it wasn't a brilliant show. For some reason I felt there was going to be an upset. And there was. When Ant and Dec announced that the second person safe was Mark there was pandemonium in the studio – no one could believe it. Sam, of course, was in shock – he just did not know how to handle the situation. Mark had used up all his nine lives. My God, this show was unpredictable. Then I looked over to Mark and Michelle. We had had 25,000 applicants – and there they were, our two finalists.

20 December – The Final

After 23 weeks on air it was now the night of the final. I was more or less resigned to the fact that Michelle would win – and therefore I relaxed and watched the show as a fan – just waiting for Michelle to pick up her crown. We had decided beforehand that the finalists would sing 'All This Time'. Simon Fuller also suggested a song called 'The Meaning Of Love' for Michelle. Mark sang 'Measure Of A Man', a song Clay Aiken had sung on *American Idol*.

I walked into the studio 10 minutes before we went live and noticed something immediately: there wasn't the same buzz there had been in the first series when Gareth and Will had fought it out. That had been special. On the night it seemed that Mark was singing to prove he deserved to be there and Michelle was singing to accept her title – it was as simple and predictable as that.

The moment they announced Michelle had won, Pete Waterman stood up and ran out of the studio. The following day the press ran a story that he had left because he didn't think Michelle should have won the competition and didn't want to appear a hypocrite. In Pete's defence, he had made it clear right from the start that he did not think Michelle was a pop idol. A good singer, yes, but he believed the show was all about finding the very best.

My opinion is that only time will tell whether or not we made the right decision. If Michelle fails to become a breakout artist, Pete will have been proved right in the sense that it could be said that Michelle won partly on a sympathy vote.

I spoke to Mark almost immediately after the result. He was calm – he had known he wasn't going to win. Michelle's family was going crazy and Michelle ended up in a bit of a daze. After I congratulated her I went to my dressing room and packed my bags.

Leaving the studio that night felt really weird. We had received more than 10 million votes and had fantastic ratings, but as far as I was concerned there was still something missing. Excitement. Outside the studio there were no fans at all; it was all deathly quiet, which I thought strange.

So I just shook hands with Neil Fox, kissed Nicki Chapman and went out to dinner with my family.

Looking back, I do believe the second series really worked. The public loved the show. The media love it, too. *Pop Idol* is very slick, well-produced television. But this time I felt it lacked passion. It was not quite enough. For me it was like having a great Chinese meal – beautifully prepared and absolutely delicious, but an hour or two later you feel a bit hungry again.

I felt I had done enough with *Pop Idol* and it was time to bring in fresh faces, a new panel of judges. I had lost my enthusiasm. The future for *Pop Idol* is quite simple – when you are auditioning for kids of a certain age it is exactly the same as fishing for cod. There comes a point when you have overfished the stocks. You have to give them time to replenish themselves. For me it had been two fun years. I was happy with my decision not to judge another series. It felt good to leave the show on a high.

Simon Says: Only Six Pop Idol Finalists Have a Chance of Success

Roxanne Over a period of about five weeks Roxanne moulded herself into a pop star. She looked and sounded the part. The problem with Roxanne is she was too good and when you are that confident the voting public thinks you don't need its help. I believe Roxanne fell into this trap. My advice to Roxanne is to use the show as a platform. Start a band and get some experience.

Susanne She must have mixed emotions. She went through a hell of a lot. She was bullied at school for being fat. She then enters the toughest talent contest in the world and makes the final five and at one point is a leading contender to win the competition. She then has to face the bullies again, thanks to someone planting that press story. It is both sad and ironic. Susanne has a unique talent but she lacked consistency. But she did have passion. She has a chance of making it and I hope she succeeds.

Chris There was a time when I was really tempted to sign Chris to my label. I had loads of people phoning me up raving about him. In the end I decided not to because of my other commitments. Of all the finalists Chris is the one who could actually make it and surprise a lot of people. He has the potential to be a really good singer.

Sam Once Sam had left the competition we had so many phone calls from so many different people. Most said he should be a star and it was unfair that he was kicked out. Fortunately Simon Fuller came on the scene and wanted Mark and Sam to be a duet, which I thought was a brilliant idea. I think they could have a good future together.

Mark Just when you think you are beginning to understand what the public wants in the music industry Mark makes the final. What can I say? I would never have predicted it. Mark is quite a good singer but nothing out of the ordinary. When I first met him I just thought, OK, you could be a good session singer – but that's it. He's not a star so the best option for him is to do that *Pop Idol* duet with Sam.

Michelle I was delighted that Michelle won the competition. She has a good voice and the personality to match. Under normal circumstances she never would have got a recording contract – that's for sure. But I don't know whether the public voted for her because she was the best, because they felt sorry for her or because she did not conform to the normal image of a pop star. All three are fine – but are sympathy votes going to sell records? She could sell millions of records – only time will tell – but if it fizzles out in a year's time then it's a problem. The good news is that Michelle had a No.1 single in February 2004; she's now a household name and she has a chance of a lifetime. Time will tell.

I Don't Mean to Be Rude, But...
If Peter Andre is Making a Record – Get Me Out of Here!

One of the funniest TV programmes I have ever watched is the most recent I'm a Celebrity – Get Me Out of Here! *Most of the comedy is unintentional and that's why I love it. The casting was inspired this year.*

The real stars were Johnny-not-so-Rotten, Lord Brocket and Jordan. I know Katie Price quite well and was pleased the audience got to see another side to her (apart from the front). I have always known her to be smart, funny and self-effacing and she has shown that really well. I also loved Johnny's walkout (the rebel!). I would remake Carry On Doctor *with Lord Brocket and I was genuinely pleased for Kerry, who I know well through Bryan from Westlife.*

But the best part of the show was Peter Andre. This guy's career was so over prior to the show it was a last-ditch effort to try and kick-start it. I just loved the way his manager had so obviously instructed him to sing at every opportunity and I'm sure this prompted Mr Rotten's early exit. One of the funniest moments was when he was singing and the others, having to listen, developed this terrible glassy expression. But Andre's best line was 'Of course I need singing lessons.'

The down side to all this is that, unfortunately, I fear he will get a record deal. Just like Mark Owen did on Celebrity

Big Brother. *Would I sign him? Not in a million years. In fact I would rather crawl through the maggot box than listen to his album.*

I predict that 2004 will prove to be the worst year for pop music since pop music was invented. It will be the year the final curtain comes down on a whole host of acts. And not before time. Over the past few years so many major record labels have made crazy decisions in signing new acts and most have been a complete waste of time.

I compare the current state of the pop market to a restaurant dessert trolley. Instead of offering diners five or six tempting desserts, imagine being offered 70 or 80 choices instead – most of which are past their sell-by date – and hidden in the middle are the real gems. That's the pop world today. There are too many mediocre artists – and most will be on the way out. Perhaps some of my artists will be among them – in any case, it has to happen.

The future of the music business today is dependent on how quickly we adapt to things going wrong. My attitude to falling record sales is that if sales are down we are clearly not giving the public what it wants.

I believe the record-buying public is getting sick to death of the constant hype and the stupid press stories about artists' private lives – all put out in the vain hope that they will generate more record sales. The most common ploy used today is that Miss X has tragically just split up with her long-standing lover; this is normally put out a week before Miss X is about to release her new single. Now tell me: is that going to sell more records? Do these people actually believe that, if you put a record out and then let it be known that the artist is now single and available, a host of love-struck, horny young boys will buy the single? Err, no...but this sort of story has become the norm.

More PR people are spinning stories to cover failure than are actually doing the job they are supposed to do – publicise the star in a positive fashion. It is quite common now for a PR campaign to be planned well in advance of a high-profile release merely to cover up the low sales anticipated. So why put the record out at all? When it comes to publicity Kym Marsh gets a bucket load – but you only have to compare her record sales to those of Dido's to understand which music the public prefers to buy.

The cost involved in putting together an album today is in the region of £1 million and that's another reason why the bloodbath will happen this year – and quite frankly I can't wait. It's time for a cull. I preferred the time when the pop market was less crowded but had bigger stars. When acts like Bros, Take That or the Spice Girls made it big they were out there on their own and it was a far more exciting time. That will come again and frankly I can't wait.

Also available in Ebury Press Paperback

To order please tick the box

Biography

Scoring at Half-Time / George Best	£6.99	☐
1979 / Rhona Cameron	£7.99	☐

Travel Writing

In Search of the Tiger / Ian Stafford	£7.99	☐
Tick Bite Fever / David Bennun	£7.99	☐
The Weekenders in Calcutta	£7.99	☐
The Weekenders in Africa	£7.99	☐
Dave Gorman's Googlewhack Adventure	£10.99	☐

FREE POST AND PACKING
Overseas customers allow £2.00 per paperback

BY PHONE: 01624 677237

BY POST: Random House Books
C/o Bookpost, PO Box 29, Douglas
Isle of Man, IM99 1BQ

BY FAX: 01624 670923

BY EMAIL: bookshop@enterprise.net

Cheques (payable to Bookpost) and credit cards accepted

Prices and availability subject to change without notice.
Allow 28 days for delivery.
When placing your order, please mention if you
do not wish to receive any additional information.

www.randomhouse.co.uk